THAT VOICE

In Search of

Ann Drummond-Grant,

the Singer Who

Shaped My Life

MARCIA MENTER

SHE WRITES PRESS

Published 2024
Printed in the United States of America

Print ISBN: 978-1-64742-662-0
E-ISBN: 978-1-64742-663-7
Library of Congress Control Number: [LOCCN]

For information, address:
She Writes Press
1569 Solano Ave #546
Berkeley, CA 94707

Interior design and typeset by Katherine Lloyd, The DESK

She Writes Press is a division of SparkPoint Studio, LLC.

Names and identifying characteristics have been changed to protect the privacy of certain individuals.

For Drummie

MOVING IMAGE

I'M WATCHING A GRAINY KINESCOPE on YouTube, hardly believing I've managed to track it down. The D'Oyly Carte Opera Company, in New York on its 1955 American tour, is performing a short version of *The Pirates of Penzance*, live, on the highbrow TV show *Omnibus*. The ladies of the chorus crowd a painted set under lighting that does not flatter their heavy stage makeup. They go through their little dance steps impeccably, hoop skirts bouncing, as they have hundreds of times before, marking the words of the songs with hand gestures and facial expressions ordained by W.S. Gilbert seventy-six years earlier.

The D'Oyly Carte Company of 1955 is *the* official Gilbert and Sullivan troupe, holder of the copyrights, keeper of the flame. I'm sure the performers have had precious little time to memorize the cuts needed to compress a two-hour comic opera into forty minutes, but nobody makes a mistake. The pickup orchestra has its scruffy moments, but the conductor, Isidore Godfrey, brings the music to life, as always. The cast is comfortable enough to mug when mugging is called for, and I mug right along with them, mouthing the words.

I'd known this footage existed for years and had a vague idea it could be viewed at the Museum of Television and Radio, but I never took myself there—that would have meant exposing a private desire. Eventually the internet, that vast public repository of private desires, led me to the firm that bought the old *Omnibus* shows. I tried to license this segment so I could watch it, but—bless them—they posted it online for free. Now its true audience, wonky and geriatric, has begun showing up, one at a time, to see a rare video record of the performers we've listened and listened to.

The cast shares three principals with the recording I grew up with. Most significantly, it has the same formidable contralto—the battleaxe as indispensable to Gilbert and Sullivan as Margaret Dumont was to the Marx Brothers. Ruth, the Pirate Maid of all Work, is played by Ann Drummond-Grant. She died before I knew she existed, but she shaped the course of my life. *I am watching Ann Drummond-Grant.*

She's fifty, about to turn fifty-one. She moves into the frame in left profile, an angle I've never seen in photographs, and not a flattering one. The enormous Jolly Roger hat surmounting a heavy wig of dark curls throws her features out of proportion: her nose looks oddly snub, her heavily shadowed eyes small under large painted brows. And her neck is beginning to sag. She points a dainty pistol at the tenor. It's the beginning of the famous Paradox Trio, in which Ruth and the Pirate King tell Frederic that because he was born on February 29, he's had only five birthdays, so he's technically five years old, not twenty-one, and must therefore remain apprenticed to the pirates. . . .

If I have to explain these plots, it will not go well for me.

She looks intent, intent, intent. Like every Ruth before her, she laughs six hearty laughs on the eighth notes of the intro, then sits down on a conveniently placed rock to begin the trio's first verse. Her voice is exactly the same as on my 1957 recording; she was known for being absolutely consistent from performance to performance, in sickness and health. As called for, she puts her hands on her hips, locking her thumbs in the wide belt of her Pirate Maid outfit (aproned hoop skirt, officer's naval jacket). She uses an actual gesture to hand off the next verse to the Pirate King, as though the audience won't be able to figure out that he's singing next. There is no line in a D'Oyly Carte performance that isn't telegraphed in some way. But her smile is lovely. Lovely. Seen full face, she is a regally beautiful woman.

There's not enough of her in this broadcast. It leaves out the song where Ruth explains how Frederic came to be a pirate (she, his slightly deaf nursemaid, was charged with apprenticing him to a *pilot*), as well as the Act I duet it took me decades to recognize as a brilliant parody of Verdi. But it's more of her than I had before, another piece of a puzzle that can never be completed. For more than fifty years since I first heard her voice, she's been lodged in my psyche, a benign presence, a lifelong friend. This has never changed because I've never spoken about her. But I need to speak about her now.

It's because of Ann Drummond-Grant that I committed myself to music school and the study of singing, even though I didn't have a fabulous voice or, more important, a bone-deep desire to perform. It's because of her that I came to understand the meaning of a private self and a private inner life, a center no one else had to be granted access to, a non-physical room of my own. She had that same understanding. Even on camera, a woman of enormous presence and discipline telling an audience all she knows, there is a certain privacy about her. And her voice, on vinyl, has the gravity of a whole soul.

Not that I listen to her on vinyl these days, though those first LPs, and the extra copies I bought to make sure I would never be without her, are on a high shelf in my apartment, having followed me through a dozen moves. I have her digitally now, on CD, in the cloud, on every one of my devices.

Vinyl—analog—is best because at some point she sang into a microphone, and the force of her voice created grooves on a physical surface. I listened to those records so many times that the grooves were burned into my brain. I know that if a surgeon touched the right place with a probe, her voice would ring out in the operating room. All I have to do to hear her is close my eyes. Not even that.

At this writing I've lived a dozen years longer than she did; she was not quite fifty-five when she died. It's startling to be older than she ever was, to see the latter part of my life plain as day in the mirror. If I'm going to tell this tale, it's time to begin.

LISTENING

I GREW UP IN SYRACUSE, NEW YORK, where it snows at least 120 inches a year—two inches one day, six the next—beginning around Halloween and ending sometime in April. When I walked to school, snowflakes gathered in the cuffs of my boots and ice crystals formed where my scarf covered my mouth; under my mittens, my hands were chapped. Puddles of water gathered by the radiator in the front hall where coats were draped to dry. Each day's snow got plowed into large dirty curbside drifts, the streets got salted, and traffic kept right on moving—no small matter in a landscape filled with the rounded glacial hills called drumlins. Southern Scotland, where Ann Drummond-Grant grew up, is likewise a land of drumlins, though there's much less snow.

I lived in the one big old house on a hilly street where little split-levels popped up like mushrooms in the 1950s. There had once been large, graceful elms, but they died of Dutch Elm disease and were cut down, leaving the street oddly bare.

My father was a physician in general practice. After office hours, he drove around in the rain and snow, making house calls. He had large deep feelings that were largely inaccessible, but I knew he loved me. My love for him was shot through with the fear of losing him. It was my father who introduced me to Gilbert and Sullivan. He loved music; we had a framed photo of him playing the violin as a boy, documenting the pride his

Jewish immigrant parents took in being able to pay for lessons. When he went to medical school, he put the violin away.

My mother *should* have worked. She was smart and decisive, a born executive. But she spent her days doing what doctors' wives did back then: having lunch, playing canasta, making reckless stabs at whatever crafts her friends were taking up. No one in her family went to college, in which respect they were like no other Jews I knew. She wasn't long out of high school when she met my father, who was interning in her hometown of Wilmington, Delaware.

Mother loved me—at the end of her life, she even said so— but not in any way I could discern. She spoke to me angrily, without patience or tenderness. I took it in stride, not knowing how else to take it. She rarely held or cuddled me; my earliest memory was of the disgust on her face as she changed my diaper. I remember exactly one time I was allowed to snuggle on her lap; I felt anxious because I was sucking my thumb and drooling on her apron. I wanted so much to love her the way I was supposed to, but never did manage it.

Mother was the oldest of eight and grew up without a speck of space to herself, which, I suppose, accounts for her possessiveness of the home turf. She tolerated no kind of messiness. My childhood friends have memories of eating cookies over the wastebasket so as not to scatter a single crumb.

She had an ear for music, though she couldn't read it. She listened to the opera broadcasts on Saturday afternoons and sang in a confident cabaret voice as she washed the dishes—pop standards from the thirties, mostly, and never a whole song. A verse, or a snatch of a verse. *Missed the Saturday dance . . . Heard they crowded the floor . . . Couldn't bear it without you. . . .*

She sang to herself. Singing, for her, was a private affair. Once when she was listening to Leontyne Price on the radio, I told her, "I can sing like that!" She said, "Okay, let's hear it."

I sang a high note in my best seven-year-old voice. She made a face and motioned me away. How could she not have heard how good I was?

I was a late child, a surprise. I had two brothers: Julian, eleven years older than me, and Robert, seven years older. Both were obsessive listeners. From the time I was tiny, I shadowed them and heard what they heard. Julian loved classical music, had perfect pitch and took piano lessons, forging his way through Chopin nocturnes on our blurry sounding upright. He never played a record just once. I remember working on a jigsaw puzzle while he listened, over and over, to Prokofiev's Second Piano Concerto. I thought it was awful, clangy and dissonant, but after a couple of hours, I liked it.

Robert played guitar and piano by ear and liked anything good. Once I stood outside his door while he listened to "It Might as Well Rain until September" a dozen times, fascinated by Carole King's unbeautiful, electronically doubled voice. Then he switched over to Zero Mostel in A Funny Thing Happened on the Way to the Forum, another unbeautiful voice I couldn't not listen to. The world had room for every kind of singer.

When I was older, I began listening to Broadway musicals on my own: Carousel, Fiddler on the Roof, Funny Girl. I seem to remember singing and dancing along with the records, but that can't be right. The stereo was downstairs in a public part of the house, and I wouldn't have sung out loud if anyone else was home. The one place I performed happily was at summer camp, hours away in the Adirondacks. I won a part in the camp show by belting out "Matchmaker, Matchmaker" from Fiddler and sang like a star in performance. At school, though, I more than once auditioned successfully for a part, only to be replaced when I couldn't make myself heard. Shyness seized me by the throat, and my voice vanished.

But I *knew* I could sing. It was one of the few things I knew for sure. I didn't know how to dress—my bunkmates at camp once did a fashion intervention to stop me from wearing plaids with florals. I didn't know how to interact in groups without being "on," believing that aggressive cleverness would make people like me. This usually backfired; most of the snarky things I said were taken the wrong way or not understood at all. I persisted. I had no other language for reaching out to people and usually missed the signals when people reached out to me. My sense of aloneness—of not being able to get through—generated an anxiety so familiar I ceased to be aware of it. But it was visible to all, in the crooks of my elbows and the backs of my knees, as eczema. I scratched my left ankle raw till I was a teenager, when finally, mercifully, I was given a tube of cortisone ointment.

3

CHUBBETTE

I WAS A PUDGY CHILD, the sort of pudge that people find adorable in babies but unacceptable when the babies grow up. I had squishy thighs and upper arms and a little pot belly; my uncle who loved to pinch baby fat found plenty to pinch on me. It would never have occurred to me that this was hereditary, but what I had was a Russian Jewish Babushka Body in training: I was built like my grandmothers, who weren't thin. It shouldn't have mattered. I was perfectly healthy. But I grew up believing that I was fat, that it was my fault, and that fat was not lovable.

I craved savory things, not sweets. I have a memory of crawling, still in diapers, to a kitchen cupboard, opening it, and swigging soy sauce from the bottle in utter bliss. But I acquired the classic American carb addiction soon enough, and while I was never obese, I was bigger than I was supposed to be. From the age of six, I was always being entreated to diet, always sneaking food, always trying to look in the mirror and see someone thin. Mother dressed me in Chubbettes, a line of dresses for little girls "on the plump side." (Tagline: "She can have a tummy . . . and still look yummy!") Whenever I saw that label, I felt humiliated.

I might have felt better about my body if I'd learned to enjoy moving it. Some of my classmates took ballet lessons and had little tutus, but I was made to understand that such things were not for me. Gym class was full of activities I was bad at. In any game of dodgeball, I was the first to be hit. I couldn't shinny up a rope or vault over a pommel horse. We weren't taught how to do those things; we just took a run at the equipment, one of us after another, and either managed it or didn't. I tried and failed for years to pull myself up onto the gymnastic rings, finally succeeding in sixth grade and yelling, "Jesus Christ!" to the consternation of my Catholic gym teacher. I hadn't realized such skills could be worked on and acquired. Nor did I understand, at age twelve, that hormones were beginning to kick in.

Puberty made everything worse in ways I had no language for. I was supposed to want breasts, but the minute they sprouted, I was supposed to keep them in check. I had a bathing suit with foam cups that were nowhere near filled; at summer camp, I stowed interesting rocks in them. One day I noticed in Mother's bedroom mirror that my waist curved in, and my hips curved out—an hourglass shape, which was supposed to be good. (I had no idea what an actual hourglass figure looked like, or that it was created by corsets.) I didn't realize it meant I was destined to be hippy, busty, and short-waisted, that I would never, ever look good in the clothes the slim, willowy girls wore. I had no real sense of my body at all, a state that persisted for decades.

Some of my classmates started menstruating in sixth grade. They seemed to sweat and suffer with it. In seventh grade, at thirteen, it was my turn. I excused myself from math class with pains radiating from somewhere under the pot belly; in the girls' bathroom, I saw dark ugly blood. I knew what it was, but it horrified me. On the way back to class, a bulky sanitary napkin stuffed in my underpants, I asked myself in a not-nice way, "How does it feel to be sexually *mature?*" I'd never had a sexual feeling that I knew of.

For reasons unknown to me, I wanted to tell Mother about getting my period before I told anyone else. It seemed fitting, though she and I had never discussed periods. So I endured a planned visit to a friend's house—the pain was intense, I was dizzy with it—before walking home. I found Mother in bed with the shades drawn. She was having a migraine, her first in many years, and in fact the only one I remember her having. She took my news with a grunt of chagrin: she didn't need this. She managed to fish a sanitary belt from her lingerie drawer and tell me where the pads were before returning to bed. If I'd thought I would be able to bond with her over this, I was wrong.

Some weeks later, she presented me with a book called *Time to Grow Up: An Affectionate Guide for Young Ladies from Ten to Sixteen* by an ex-pinup girl called Candy Jones. Ms. Jones was indeed affectionate, but I was not one of the young ladies she had in mind. Her basic assumptions were that "every girl wants to get married and raise a family," which I didn't, and that jobs were something "to pass the time before the right marrying man shows up," which I thought would never happen to me. (Jones herself married twice, worked all her life, and claimed, plausibly, to have been hypnotized and used as a spy by the CIA.)

Time to Grow Up had been published in 1962, and by the time I encountered it in 1966, it was hilariously out of date. While Betty Friedan was writing *The Feminine Mystique*, Candy Jones was hoping that a woman would never become president of the United States: "Confidentially and just between the two of us, do you think one of us actually could run this country without getting everything bollixed up and forgetting to turn off the gas at the White House when we went on vacation?" I didn't know enough to feel insulted by this.

I did know girls who might have appreciated Jones's thirteen-point checklist for determining whether your clothes fit properly, who might have nodded and smiled when informed that a strapless white formal can be accented with an emerald-green satin clutch. These were the same slender girls who knew how to talk to boys and liked the idea of dating them, and who gave parties where people made out. I couldn't imagine this. Didn't want to.

The sole sentence from *Time to Grow Up* that stayed with me was this: "Some girls awaken to the fact that their stomach looks like a football in a fitted princess line dress." That was a figure flaw—any extra flesh was a figure flaw—fixable by sit-ups, leg lifts, and a panty girdle. I never did fix it. Even now, when Pilates has given me a rock-solid core, I still have a football stomach. *Candy Jones lied to me.*

This, then, was the adolescent girl who heard Ann Drummond-Grant's voice for the first time: shy on the inside, stocky and snarky on the outside. An introvert in extrovert's clothing—at odds with her body and so lonely she didn't even know it. Not the first or last girl of this description, surely.

4

KATISHA

ON A COLD, DARK NIGHT toward the end of 1966, my father brought home a recording of *The Mikado* and handed it to me, saying he thought I'd like it, that it was "fun." Looking at the photo on the cover—the full cast standing onstage in out-of-register color, their makeup a garish yellow—I was unimpressed. The albums I liked were slicker. The Beatles' *Revolver* had come out that year, and I'd stared at the black-and-white Klaus Voormann collage on the cover while Robert played the songs twice. But *The Mikado* was a present from my adored father, so I took it seriously.

I knew almost nothing about Gilbert and Sullivan except that they were old and English. That suited me. I'd read the Sherlock Holmes stories and mostly forgotten them, but retained a fondness for the Victorian way of saying things, in long, convoluted sentences packed with words whose meanings I might deduce if I was too lazy to look them up.

The Mikado dates from Sherlock Holmes's day, 1885. It's set in Japan, but Gilbert's Japan is England with an exotic veneer, an excuse to put his players in gorgeous costumes and have them gesture extravagantly with fans. For many years, audiences saw nothing wrong with Caucasian actors wearing yellow makeup to signify Japanese-ness. Now it's cringeworthy, and the opera has become problematic. That's a pity, because aside from its casual Victorian racism, *The Mikado* is a work of genius. I loved it from the start.

Sullivan's music was glorious, every bar of it. Gilbert's lyrics required my keen attention. (Fortunately, there was a printed libretto.) His rhymes were intricate and endlessly inventive, involving strange new words I thought I was supposed to know—like "ablutioner," to rhyme with "executioner." (It's not a real word. The opera's supreme snob, Pooh-Bah, calls a ragged stranger a "very imperfect ablutioner," meaning he doesn't bathe. It took me *years* to pick up on that.)

I wanted to memorize those words, to claim their cleverness. This being a well-crafted entertainment, there was just enough of the right sort of repetition to push the songs into my brain. The recording left out the dialogue between musical numbers, so I didn't get the whole crazy plot, but I got the gist of it, which was that these were Brits pretending to be Japanese with equal parts silliness and solemnity. The tenor was to be beheaded for no good reason; the soprano was to be buried alive, ditto; and neither was in the slightest danger of these things actually happening. Everyone was having a marvelous time, and I was invited to have one too.

My *Mikado*, a two-LP set from 1957, may be the best on record. The cast has no weak links, not always the case with the D'Oyly Carte. The sound is superb—it was the first stereo album issued by London Records, and it gave me a sense of stepping into another world. I disappeared into it. The minute the record hit the turntable, I was gone.

The Mikado was not a great leap from the Broadway musicals I'd been listening to. American musical theater is directly descended from G&S, and every lyricist from Cole Porter to Lin-Manuel Miranda has looked back to Gilbert with some combination of idolatry and competitiveness. Sheldon Harnick said that his lyrics for "Tevye's Dream" in *Fiddler on the*

Roof ("What woman is this/ by righteous anger shaken?") were inspired by Katisha's entrance in *The Mikado*.

Ah. Katisha.

Katisha is the contralto, the battleaxe, the rejected older woman—older, to Gilbert, being somewhere around forty-seven. Her entrance, at the end of Act I, is spectacular. She crashes into a scene of general rejoicing like a thunderbolt, singing at the top of her voice: "Your revels cease! Assist me, all of you!" The revels cease.

The Katisha on my recording was Ann Drummond-Grant. It was, she once admitted, her favorite role, and I've never heard anyone sing it better. But I have no memory of hearing her for the first time. Her voice didn't leap out and throttle me, as it has so many times since.

Nor was I conscious of what sets the role of Katisha apart from everyone else in the opera, and from all other G&S contralto roles: she is permitted to express a deep, private sorrow—not once, but twice. For most of the opera she portrays, gleefully, a perfect gorgon. But in these two numbers, the action stops, and she bares a broken human heart. Some part of me responded to this.

I can't say how many hearings it took before I began to experience Katisha as the heart and soul of the opera, its gravitational center. Objectively speaking, she's not. But this particular Katisha had a presence that somehow drew everything toward her. Her voice was rich and impassioned, the low notes deep and dark, the high notes shining. I scarcely took note that I, too, was being drawn toward her. I only knew I had a new world to escape to, and she was in it.

5

PIRAMIKAFORE

GILBERT AND SULLIVAN IS AN INSTITUTION. Its acolytes are like small children who want their favorite bedtime stories told exactly the same way each night. At a performance of any of the operas, a large portion of the audience will be mouthing the words—and if any lyric is "updated," a shudder will go through the crowd. Occasional productions may change the setting, but they mustn't change the operas. You could say the same of a Beethoven symphony: however the conductor fiddles with it, it has to be Beethoven.

Now, in equating Gilbert and Sullivan with Beethoven, I'm committing a cardinal error I wouldn't have understood at thirteen. Americans think G&S is highbrow because of its intricate rhymes, polysyllabic words, and utter Englishness. For us, it's the meat of the elite. But for the British, it's distinctly middlebrow—hoary Victorian stuff, entertainment for people who have pretensions to culture but don't want to think about it too hard. I've heard more than one British musician get defensive about loving G&S.

As a thirteen-year-old American girl, I believed I was entering a rarefied cultural sphere when I sat down with *The Mikado*. Nobody I knew was listening to this stuff. People my age listened to rock, and as I got older, the rock got harder: Pink Floyd, Led Zeppelin, The Rolling Stones. Loud, angry, sexy music. *The Mikado* was none of those things, though I cranked up the volume when no one was home. It was militantly lighthearted, and I needed that.

Gilbert, I have long thought, was the epitome of Pre-Freudian Man. He wouldn't have dreamed of searching for demons within himself or anyone else. His characters are benign, even when they're talking about boiling someone in oil. And he never, ever wrote about sex—never, to cadge a line from *Patience*, wrote a single word "calculated to bring the blush of shame to the cheek of modesty." That line gets a laugh, but Gilbert meant it. His mission was to make the theater respectable for a family audience, which it hadn't been. In the long history of the D'Oyly Carte Company—founded by Richard D'Oyly Carte, the impresario who brought Gilbert and Sullivan together in 1875—the ladies never showed their legs, let alone their cleavage. The word *breast* referred to the heart, the seat of feeling. That was a breast I could relate to.

Not long after I started listening to *The Mikado*, my father brought home its companion recording from 1957, *The Pirates of Penzance*. I didn't like it as much but soon warmed to it. It shared most of its cast with *The Mikado*, so the players were familiar to me and felt like friends. Soon they would be family.

The first friend I encountered after the opening chorus of pirates (drinking sherry, which I didn't know was funny) was Ann Drummond-Grant—she of the hyphenated name—as Ruth, the pirates' maid.

Ruth is even more a figure of cruel fun than Katisha. She loves Frederic, whom she mistakenly apprenticed to the pirates as a small boy, and has convinced him that she's young and beautiful, though she is in fact (wait for it) forty-seven. When he sees a chorus of young ladies approaching in the distance, the scales fall from his eyes, and he renounces her. There ensues a ridiculous scene sung with utter seriousness. It's also a truly operatic scene, and when I saw Verdi's *Il Trovatore* many years later, I finally understood what Sullivan was spoofing. Ann Drummond-Grant had the voice for it. She could have sung Verdi, but I didn't yet know what that meant.

There were other numbers in *Pirates* that I liked better, including a showstopper where Sullivan has the women and men sing two completely different choruses that combine gorgeously into one. It's one of his favorite tricks. He taught me about counterpoint before I knew what counterpoint was.

Then there were the words. So many words. I felt compelled to learn them, even the ones I didn't understand—as when the Modern Major General sings:

> I quote in elegiacs all the crimes of Heliogabalus
> In conics I can floor peculiarities parabolous. . . .

Other Victorian lyricists indulged in this sort of frenetic wordplay, but nobody did it better than Gilbert. Most of his satire was lost on me, but I found plenty in *Pirates* to love. When a work is good, it's good on many levels.

I started listening to the two operas in sequence and soon asked my father for a third. He brought me *HMS Pinafore*, Gilbert and Sullivan's first monster hit. These three operas, known collectively by fans as PiraMikaFore, are the most popular, at least in the US. A less obsessive listener might have stopped there.

My *Pinafore*, from 1959, was the next in the London Stereo series. I noted two major differences in this recording. The first was that Ann Drummond-Grant wasn't on it. In her place, in the contralto role of Little Buttercup, was someone named Gillian Knight.

The other difference was the inclusion of the spoken dialogue, which was funny and helpful for understanding the plot. After multiple listenings, though, it started to seem like a series of interruptions to the music, and I can't say I needed to hear it over and over, especially since it was delivered in the stilted manner that marked all D'Oyly Carte performances. Still, I memorized it and decided that speaking in a stilted manner was a fine thing. It was a way to stand out, and I wanted to stand out because I didn't fit in.

Pinafore is a pleasure—sprightly, tuneful, brisk as a hornpipe. I'd seen a local production once and knew about Little Buttercup, who is plump and pleasing and bears a Dark Secret, and about the self-satisfied Captain, whose claim to fame is that he never gets seasick or swears. I knew about the Common Sailor who loves above his station, and the First Lord of the Admiralty, who loves (the same lass) below his. All very silly and tame to an American girl with no understanding of the British class system being surgically skewered by Gilbert. But then, I had no understanding of my own country's caste system, which was staring me in the face.

6

BLACK GIRLS

I NEVER ASKED MYSELF WHY a teenage girl who could pass for normal—who'd even decided which Beatle she had a crush on (George, then John)—would seize so eagerly and passionately on a bunch of sex-free Victorian entertainments. For the next three years, I lived a double life. In the larger life, the inner life, I became intimately familiar with eleven Gilbert and Sullivan operas—all of them except for the first, which is mostly lost, and the last two, which are seldom produced. In my smaller, outer life, I used the operas as an invisible shield. I needed one. I didn't know who I was or how to be.

I entered puberty and junior high at the same time, and both were foreign countries. I was increasingly conscious of having too much flesh to be considered attractive, just when I was supposed to want a boyfriend. But I *didn't* want one. If there was a magic spell that would render me boy-crazy, it hadn't yet been cast.

Worse than the boy thing was the culture shock. My elementary school had been almost completely white: there was exactly one Black child in my class, from the one Black family in the district. The junior high was much larger, with many Black students bused in from the other side of town. It was the first year of an experiment in forced integration, and it was tough on everyone.

BLACK GIRLS

I was incapable of seeing my Black classmates as being like me because I'd been raised to believe they weren't. There was an understanding in my family that people of color were inferior. If Mother saw a heavy Black woman, she'd say: "Look at *that!*"—as though the woman were not a person but a thing. My father had Black patients on Medicaid who were deemed somehow responsible for their economic distress. His Yiddish-speaking parents had owned a dry-cleaning plant where they employed people they called *schvartzes*, a term of contempt. Schvartzes, they said, were ruining the old neighborhood, which had been a Jewish ghetto before it was a Black one. I was ten when that neighborhood was split by an interstate highway and left for dead.

An African American woman named Mary Franklin worked for my mother when I was little. She was poor; she was heavy; she was kind; my brothers made fun of the way she spoke. Once she tried to explain to me that God had made people in different colors just as he made tulips in different colors. He made pink tulips and brown tulips. While Mary was saying this, she was pressing sheets on the mangle iron in the tiny pantry behind the kitchen. The scent of clean laundry mingled with her own clean musky scent: *was this how brown tulips smelled?* No one in my family believed that brown tulips were as good as pink ones. The serenity with which I accepted this is shocking to me now.

The Black girls in my seventh-grade class scared the shit out of me. They seemed older. Tougher. One girl asked me point blank, out of nowhere, if I was a Jew. I responded—primly, as I'd been instructed in Sunday school—that I was a Jew and proud of it. She shot back, "I didn't ask if you was *proud* of it." And she was right—it was a dumb answer. If you have to say you're proud of something, you probably aren't.

The Black girls were absolutely in their bodies, even the heavier ones—I hadn't known it was okay to be comfortable with being heavy. Some of those girls could *sing*. They had grownup voices, focused and penetrating, unlike my sweet wavery one; they sang Motown hits and sounded like the real thing. At Christmas, our art teacher had us make papier-mâché angels and spray-paint them gold. The Black girl with the best singing voice, who was also named Marcia, said she wanted to make a Supreme, as in Diana Ross and The Supremes. I thought that was a cool idea but felt contempt because I was pretty sure she had no intention of executing it. I liked The Supremes—we all did. But I couldn't relate to this other Marcia who liked them too.

The things I felt confident about—being a good student, knowing big words—suddenly meant nothing. I tried to sound smart but came out sounding patronizing. Once, between classes, a Black girl who'd been nice to me took a lipstick and smudged a red smear across my left breast as she walked past. I might have said—anything. I might have engaged with her in *any* way. But I felt a judgment had been passed—I was quick to feel that—and burrowed into being humiliated. Damn those breasts! It was a favorite dress. Would the lipstick come out? Would I have to tell my mother how it got there? (I never did, nor did I wear the dress again.)

I didn't know how to relate to any of my new classmates. So I did that thing kids do when they enter a new school: hoped I had a clean slate, hoped nobody would know I was uncool, though I had been uncool for years and anyone could see it. I set about trying to figure out which of the kids I was better than. Or at least smarter than. I had to know who to look down on.

I felt okay about myself twice a week, in music class, where we sat at our desks and sang as our teacher played the piano. I sang in tune, and my voice stood out clearly. One of the songs was "Carefully on Tiptoe Stealing" from *Pinafore*. On my recording, it sounded completely different from the arrangement for school kids. My real music education happened at home, by the stereo.

7

THAT VOICE

My fourth Gilbert and Sullivan opera was *Iolanthe*. It was an older recording and sounded darker, like it had been produced in a cave. The cast was new to me, but there was one familiar name: Ann Drummond-Grant, in the title role.

Unlike the operas I knew that opened with hearty men's choruses—Sailors, Pirates, Gentlemen of Japan—*Iolanthe* opened with "dainty little fairies" singing a chorus that sounded like Mendelssohn's *A Midsummer Night's Dream*, though I didn't catch the reference. Gilbert's words were as tart as Sullivan's music was sweet: "Tripping hither, tripping thither, / Nobody knows why or whither. . . ."

I might have wondered what those fairies were doing in a grownup opera, tromping around their fairy ring without knowing why. Gilbert's audience would have recognized them as coming right out of Christmas pantomimes, the singing, dancing, slapstick extravaganzas that are popular even now: fairytale entertainments for British children, laced with bawdy double entendres for their parents.

Gilbert's stroke of satirical genius was setting his fairies in opposition to the dukes, earls, and baronets of the House of Lords, rendering them, too, as pantomime figures—wealthy, privileged, and not very bright. The Peers march onstage to the sound of trumpets and drums, dressed in ermine-trimmed robes and coronets, singing lines with a little too much truth in them:

> Bow, bow, ye lower middle classes!
> Bow, bow, ye tradesmen, bow, ye masses!

Their boss, the Lord Chancellor, has one of the most daunting patter songs in G&S, recounting a nightmare that gets crazier and crazier yet makes perfect sense. Generations of baritones have dreaded losing their way in it. On my LP it was sung by Martyn Green, who made it sound easy. Shortly after recording it, he left the D'Oyly Carte Company in a fit of pique. I didn't know about that, or about how big a star he was, or that he would soon cross my path in person. But I could see he was an excellent Lord Chancellor, conveying the character with every inflection of every word. G&S is not deep, but its performers have to be. They have to treat their roles with utter sincerity, especially in the silly places, or the magic will vanish.

Every bit of *Iolanthe* is good. It may be my favorite opera, though I've always been determined not to have a favorite. Sullivan wrote some of the fairies' music in the style of Wagner, whose *Ring* cycle had premiered in London earlier that year (1882); the original Fairy Queen was dressed like Brünnhilde. There are layers and layers of allusion in *Iolanthe*, all of which were lost on me. No matter. I adored it.

The Fairy Queen was one of Ann Drummond-Grant's signature roles, but she never recorded it. I wish she had. She did record the role of Iolanthe, and it changed my life.

Iolanthe has been banished for marrying a mortal; her sister fairies beg their queen to summon her from exile. There's a mysterious English horn solo as she rises out of a stream, "clad in water-weeds." And then she sings. I remember clearly the first time I heard Ann Drummond-Grant's voice rise out of the dark cave of that recording in Iolanthe's first lines:

With humbled breast and every hope laid low,
To thy behest, offended Queen, I bow.

Those words kind of die on the printed page, don't they? I had no idea what "behest" meant. But the voice was thrilling: rich and clear, with a quick vibrato. A youthful voice. A voice of emotional experience. I took a breath and held it.

I think that was the moment I was gone forever on that voice.

The illustration on the album cover showed a slim, red-haired Iolanthe hovering, wand in hand, over an Arcadian shepherd and shepherdess, the opera's matched pair of lovers. I spent a lot of time daydreaming about this. Did Ann Drummond-Grant have red hair? Was she slim? Was this how she looked when she played the part?

I didn't know that she never played the part, or that her appearance on this recording was not universally applauded. Iolanthe is a soubrette role, written for a mezzo-soprano. Some soubrette roles in G&S are saucy all the way through, like Pitti-Sing in *The Mikado*. But some, like Iolanthe, have scenes that require vocal and dramatic power. In 1951, when my recording was made, Ann Drummond-Grant was about to become the company's principal contralto, and she had power to spare. No one would see that she was a tall, stocky woman of not quite forty-seven.

Thus I heard, toward the end of the opera, the scene where Iolanthe pleads with the Lord Chancellor for her son's sake—another of Gilbert's serious moments—sung by an extraordinary voice: not the charming, slender mezzo that theater audiences of the day would have encountered, but a full-throated, shining sound that carried words and music to another level. The sound of a woman giving everything she had. Perhaps it was a bigger voice than the part really calls for. I never thought so. To me, it was that gravitational force bending everything toward it.

Here I'm supposed to say something like, "I made up my mind I wanted to sing like that." That's not what happened. What happened was that I woke to a recognition that this voice—this woman—was a friend to me. That the very sound was a core of truth and a place of shelter. Transmitted as vibration through time and space was a sense of personhood, hers and mine. I overlaid it with a certain adolescent melodrama, but it was sacred, and I knew the sacred when I met it.

Over the next few years, her voice became the center of my life and my life plan. I would join the D'Oyly Carte Company and come under the wing of Ann Drummond-Grant. The more I intuited that this wasn't possible, the more I blocked the intuition.

Those junior high school years were dark. Syracuse was dark—*dreich*, as the Scots say; it seemed always to be raining or snowing. The school was the same distance from my house as the elementary school, three-quarters of a mile, but this walk was mostly uphill, and it felt like a sentence. What lay at the end of it? A thousand ways to not fit in.

I walked to school with my friend Nina, whom I'd known since second grade, or my friend Joby, whom I'd known since we were four: smart, articulate girls who were perfectly happy to be themselves and no one else. Sometimes I walked by myself in the miserable snow, my legs red from the tops of my boots to halfway up my thighs. (Pantyhose were useless in the cold. Mine were always full of runs.) I trudged a track others had made across a vacant lot, walking in time to music from *Iolanthe*:

> We are Peers of highest station,
> Paragons of legislation,
> Pillars of the British nation!
> Tantantara! Tzing! Boom!

I was in love with the counterpoint Sullivan wrote for those lines. Replaying his music in my head was a kind of communion, almost a kind of mysticism. But music is a mystery that can be broken into its component parts and understood in the body and mind. It's a mystery one can own.

During my days at a school where my supposed advantages did not result in people liking or understanding me (or vice versa), I walked the halls armored with clever Victorian words and plush Victorian music. On weekends and occasional stolen afternoons, I sat by the stereo. I made a practice of hearing the operas in the order I had acquired them, one per day: *The Mikado. Pirates. Pinafore. Iolanthe. The Gondoliers. The Yeomen of the Guard. The Sorcerer. Patience. Ruddigore. Princess Ida. Trial By Jury.*

Wait. I'm getting the order wrong. This was my litany, and I've forgotten it. Now I think of the operas the way everyone else does, in the order they were written, starting with *Trial* and ending with *Gondoliers*. I learned them all. At some point I bypassed my father and started buying the records myself. Ann Drummond-Grant was on six of them, in four contralto roles and two soubrette roles. In ninth grade, the last year of junior high, she was far and away the most important person in my life. I never mentioned her name to a soul.

I told my parents I wanted singing lessons but didn't say why.

8

MISS PINNELL

MY FATHER ASKED HIS COUSIN Sid to recommend a voice teacher. Sid Novak was the cantor at our temple, and he sang the liturgy as though it were opera, which improved it. The music at our Reform synagogue was overblown and undistinguished, straight out of nineteenth-century Germany, where Reform Judaism began. It was more than a bit churchy; there was a large pipe organ. But I liked it. My ears could make sense of it. In my paternal grandmother's Orthodox synagogue, there was no music, only the cacophony of prayers chanted by the men at a hundred different rates. The word *brouhaha* comes from the sound of such prayers, many of which begin "*baruch haba*" (Blessed is he. . . .) or "*baruch atah*" (Blessed art Thou. . . .). The women sat in back. Their voices barely registered.

Cousin Sid had a well-trained baritone voice amplified to a large richness in the synagogue. Perhaps it wasn't so big; perhaps it was a bit dry. But he knew how to use it. When he sang the Kiddush on Friday nights, I wanted to cheer. He knew the Syracuse music scene inside and out, and suggested I study with Ruth Pinnell, a professor of voice at the Syracuse University School of Music.

The university was literally and figuratively the center of town. To a large extent, it was the reason there *was* a music scene in Syracuse—not just because of the music school, but because of all the professors, especially in math and science, who loved classical music. They wanted to live in a city with a symphony orchestra and a chamber music society, and Syracuse had both, though the orchestra was of the scrappy, scruffy sort. Families like mine had access to good music teachers; the best players in the high school band studied with professors on the Hill—University Hill, actually a whole bunch of hills, one higher than the next.

The SU School of Music was (and still is) housed in Crouse College, an enormous Victorian castle of red sandstone surmounting a particularly high hill. It was to this castle, which I had never entered, that I made my pilgrimage to sing for Miss Pinnell. Mother drove me there. She never complained about ferrying me to my various music lessons or paying for them. It was the only form of support she gave me, but now that I think about it, it wasn't small.

Was it snowing that day? I can't remember. But Crouse seemed even more romantic to me with snow flying around it, its Gothic bell tower piercing the sky—a windswept citadel of music far above the drab city. Crouse was built in 1889. Its drafty studios had high ceilings, tall windows, and transoms above the doors, through which you could hear lessons in progress. (Brouhaha, indeed.)

Miss Pinnell's studio was on the first floor in the back, behind the ornately carved split staircase guarded by a life-size plaster copy of the Winged Victory of Samothrace. It was a long room with windows on two sides, large enough to swallow a grand piano and heavy desk and still leave space for an audience. It had a tatty oriental carpet ringed with folding chairs. Like many rooms in Crouse, it could make a small voice sound large. My voice *was* small, a girl's true soprano. But I believed it was good—it had to be. My future depended on it.

Miss Pinnell was a well upholstered woman of fifty with

roller-set gray hair and bifocals—women of fifty were older in those days. Her features were strong and her manner plain and Midwestern. When I sang for her, without accompaniment, she dodged the question of teaching me. "You're too young to start lessons," she said. "The voice is still developing. Come back when you're sixteen"—I was fourteen—"and sing for me again. In the meantime, you'll need to develop some facility at the piano." Thus ended the consultation.

To Miss Pinnell's lukewarm assessment, which scarcely wavered in all the years I knew her, I responded with a zeal to win her over. I wanted to sing; she was the teacher of choice; therefore I would do whatever it took to please her. The fact that this strategy had failed to work on my mother, a woman of the same age and standoffishness, was lost on me. I knew only that I needed to start piano lessons.

I loved the piano, having grown up listening to my brother Julian's records and Julian himself. I'd taken lessons during elementary school with a nervous teacher who drove to our house in a tiny gray car and chain-smoked for half an hour. I thought he came by his nervousness honestly, a serious pianist forced to teach bratty kids like me who didn't practice. Now I wanted to practice.

We found, somehow, a teacher named Sheva Tannenbaum who mostly taught young children and was in every respect a nice lady. She gave lessons in her home, which was at the top of another damn hill, a really high one that gave my mother fits all winter. Mrs. Tannenbaum and I liked each other. She liked having an older, smarter student who was motivated to learn, and I liked being taught by someone warm and supportive. With her I could let down my guard, stop worrying about whether I was likable, and just enjoy sharing a keyboard. She started me with really easy pieces and was liberal with her praise. That's how you teach little kids, but I had never been a little kid; I'd been a smartass from the start. It was good, so good, not to have to be one now. When I showed up doubled over with menstrual cramps, she sympathized. "It gets better after you have children," she told me. "I've had three, and I'm bigger than a well down there." I blushed at this. It was the sort of useful information no grown woman had shared with me before. (I never did have children. I always had cramps, and always hated them, though I eventually gained access to better drugs for the pain.)

I practiced ninety minutes a day at our ancient upright piano, which sounded out of tune even when it wasn't but had a nice, easy action. Every session seemed to bring me closer to fulfilling my grand plan of joining the D'Oyly Carte. And when I practiced—wonder of wonders—I got better. This was the first time I understood what practicing meant. Mrs. Tannenbaum told me, and she only had to say it once, that even the little pieces I was playing could be made better by playing them with feeling. I could build a phrase, tell a story. I was given permission to make music.

And there was evening, and there was morning, and it was the end of ninth grade and junior high.

9

ANNIE, MAD MABEL, AND HARRIET THE SPY

It was 1968. Huge things happened that year, but they felt normal. The assassinations of Martin Luther King and Bobby Kennedy hardly surprised me; after President Kennedy was shot, it had seemed to me that every public figure had a target on his head. We all had targets on our heads. Why else would the people up the street have dug a fallout shelter?

I barely understood the war in Vietnam, which colored everything. My brother Robert was drafted but managed to get deferred because of a cyst on his spine. Huge relief. But then my father, a World War II veteran, accused him of being unpatriotic. Huge fight. Daddy believed that a billion Chinese would overrun Southeast Asia if we didn't hold the line in Vietnam. Nobody my age believed that.

My generation was angry, and the anger was rocket fuel. Even I was energized by it. But I was hiding out in the distant past, which seemed far more real than the world I was ostensibly living in. No one who saw me that year saw all of me.

I wanted to study Latin in high school because Daddy said it was the best way to understand English. (He was always pointing out the Latin roots of words, and though I bridled at this, and at his constant recourse to the giant Webster's

Second Unabridged sitting open on its reading stand—every moment was a teachable moment for him—I absorbed the idea that Latin was essential.) The high school I was entering had a legendary Latin teacher, but too few students had signed up for her first-year class. We were told we could take Latin I that summer and go directly into Latin II in the fall.

Thus it was that I found myself being ferried across town every morning to Corcoran High on the West Side, which might have been Timbuktu for anything I knew about it. Only now does my lack of curiosity about my birth city strike me as odd. I kept to my neighborhood, which abutted the affluent suburbs to the east. Most of what happened in my life happened somewhere along East Genesee Street, which became West Genesee Street and a foreign country when it crossed Salina Street downtown—Salina Street being named for the salt springs that once made Syracuse the greatest salt producer in the country.

Corcoran was a blocky modern structure with windowless classrooms. Mother drove me there with my friend Anne, who lived up the street. Anne's parents refused to carpool; they were writers of young adult fiction who shut themselves in their room all day to work, leaving Anne and her siblings to cadge rides as they could. Mother expressed resentment at this, but not in front of Anne.

I'd become friends with Anne after meeting her at the bus station downtown, where she hung out at the Economy Book Store. I was probably visiting the main library, borrowing and re-borrowing books on Gilbert and Sullivan, memorizing every word and burning the photos into my brain. Or I might have been haunting the old E.W. Edwards department store on Salina Street, where I pawed through D'Oyly Carte recordings and bought them one by one.

Anne was soft-spoken and subversively smart, with wire

rimmed glasses and wavy, honey-colored hair that fell every which way. She wore hand-me-down sweaters with style; I liked her on sight. Her family had recently moved from Bear Street on the North Side, a working-class neighborhood in another unknown-to-me part of town. (Italians and Poles lived on the North Side, and there was a German restaurant my father liked.) Her parents were New York Jews who had once been communists; her brother Joe was named after Stalin, though this was no longer talked about.

Anne and I got on well. I loved that her name was Anne (albeit with an "e" at the end) and that she drew obsessively with a Rapidograph pen. She drew faces that bordered on caricature but expressed entire secret lives, making up stories to go with them. She was a serious reader who arranged books chromatically—by color—on her shelves. I called her Annie, and she called me Mabel, and sometimes Mad Mabel. I angled for these nicknames but didn't tell her they were from G&S. Mabel is the soprano heroine of *The Pirates of Penzance*, and Mad Margaret is the soubrette in *Ruddigore*, sung on my recording by Ann Drummond-Grant.

Annie and I both loved *Harriet the Spy*, the children's novel about an eleven-year-old who jots down observations about her classmates and is ostracized when her notebook is found and read. Ignoring the tale's cautionary aspect, we both bought dime-store spiral notebooks and started writing. Anne drew as much as she wrote; I wrote nonstop—in Latin class, where I should have been paying better attention, or anywhere I found myself with a spare moment. I wrote because I was in love with my singer and couldn't talk about it. I wrote about wanting time to be alone with my recordings and how beautiful they were and how lucky I was to have them. I analyzed Gilbert's characters—such analyses couldn't go deep—and stood up for less popular operas like *Princess*

Ida which I thought (and still think) particularly beautiful. I wrote about every word Ann Drummond-Grant ever sang and every part she played, using the word *perfection* quite a lot, but I filled many pages before I could bring myself to write her name. Once I started writing it, I couldn't stop. I decided that because it was such a long name and usually wound up on two lines, broken somewhere in the middle, I would always give it a line of its own.

I tried to figure out why, when my friends were having crushes on boys, I had a crush on a grown woman who played a Pirate Maid and a Japanese harridan. Was there something wrong with me? After a long phone conversation with Anne about whether it was possible to love someone without feeling physical desire (I left out the part about the someone being a woman), I decided I was okay: I was feeling devotion, the sort of devotion Carl Sandburg felt for Lincoln.

No, it was love, large and life changing. I haven't parsed it yet. I've long since stopped trying.

I liked Latin, despite my imperfect attention in class. Nouns had different endings depending on the work they did in a sentence. A noun ended one way if it was the subject, another way if it was the direct object, still another if it was the indirect object. Those endings had to be memorized, but the real work was understanding what subjects and objects were in the first place. The parts of English speech I hadn't understood in junior high became clear in Latin class.

Based on that first semester, I thought Latin would be easy. I still believed that being smart meant knowing things without having to work at learning them. And in truth, I didn't know how to work. The world was like sixth-grade gym class, divided into things I could and couldn't do. I could memorize the declensions and conjugations of first-year Latin but didn't understand the discipline it took to learn a language. I could get better at a piano piece by playing it over and over but didn't know how to make it good—or even what *good* meant.

My energy that summer—the summer I turned fifteen—went into loving and being loved. I loved Gilbert and Sullivan; listening to Ann Drummond-Grant felt like being loved. Buried somewhere in all this was the sexual energy I bristled with but resisted.

No one in my circle knew what was preoccupying me. I remember an afternoon when my friend Robin demonstrated the art of French kissing on a Hostess Ho Ho, a cylindrical chocolate snack cake filled with cream. We all followed suit—it's nice to stick your tongue into a Ho Ho—but I was not about to try it with a boy. Nor were the boys in our circle, who seemed so young and unformed, about to try it with me. I was happy to be the eccentric, flamboyant, non-rock-and-roll-loving sidekick with a strange passion for violets. Robin joked that Violet must be the name of my secret boyfriend, since I was clearly not interested in the boys we knew.

No, *violet* was a word sung by my secret girlfriend—in *Ruddigore*, the opera that came directly after *The Mikado* and wasn't nearly as successful. Though of course I loved every word and note.

Ruddigore is a parody of Victorian stage melodrama. It has a priggishly virtuous heroine who brandishes her etiquette book like a bible, a baronet forced into bad behavior by a witch's curse, and a bunch of dead ancestors who step out of their portrait frames to torment him. And it has Mad Margaret, who comes onstage "wildly dressed in picturesque tatters" and declares herself unhinged by love.

Mad Margaret's song, about a violet (three syllables drawn out melodramatically) yearning to be picked by someone who chooses "wanton roses" instead, is not far from drivel. Borrowed drivel, since it harks back to Goethe's similar, subtler German lyric which Mozart set and every young soprano sings. But Sullivan treats the scene with seriousness and pathos. And on my recording, Ann Drummond-Grant—once more stepping into a soubrette role she never performed—sings it with her whole heart. Reviews of this recording tend to treat her performance as a drawback; there's nothing soubrette-like about it. But her full, rich sound galvanized me. Every inflection of every word, the truth of the emotion, and the glory of the voice itself, spoke to me. When I said I loved violets, I was talking about her.

10

DEAR MISS CARTE

THAT JULY, A SYNDICATED COLUMN in the Syracuse paper reported that the D'Oyly Carte Company was coming to New York in November. I told my father I had to see them, though normally I didn't bring him into my private world. He offered to take me—not to see every opera in the repertoire, as I wanted, but one or two. This was generous, considering that my request had been more of a demand.

The column said the company had signed with Sol Hurok, the only impresario whose name I knew. So I looked up his New York office and wrote to him, asking where I could write to Bridget D'Oyly Carte, granddaughter of Richard D'Oyly Carte, who now ran the company. They provided an address, and I sent her a letter. I still can't believe I did this. My notebook says only that the letter "was dramatic to an almost Bernhardt degree." From what I can remember, that's an understatement.

My letter said that I loved the operas and that my dream was to sing with the D'Oyly Carte. And, in an afterthought that was nothing of the kind, that I admired Miss Ann Drummond-Grant and very much hoped to write to her. Once my letter was in the mail (addressed to Miss Carte at The Savoy Hotel, 1 Savoy Hill, WC2, London) there was nothing I could do to retrieve or rephrase it. It was gone, to my nervous elation. I had to get on with my summer, and with Latin class, where I filled page after page of my note-book with Gilbert's patter songs.

Soon after mailing the letter, I had a vivid dream: An actress I admired had been shot, and I asked to be alone so I could cry. The senselessness of her death affected me far more than the deaths of the Kennedys and Martin Luther King, and I resolved to go into deep mourning.

I didn't dwell on the dream, distracted by a Latin test and my ongoing struggle to find time to listen to my operas. I'd made a religious ritual of this. The house had to be empty—I could no longer listen if Mother was home—and I'd tell my friends I was busy so they wouldn't call. But call they did, endlessly, just to talk, and I couldn't say, "I'm listening to *Patience*—please leave me alone."

Nor could I begin to explain *Patience*, in which a chorus of rapturous maidens swoon over a fleshly poet named Reginald Bunthorne, who really cares nothing for poetry but seeks only to be admired. Bunthorne loves a dairymaid named Patience, who thinks his verses are nonsense. (They are.)

To understand *Patience*, I'd had to learn that a "fleshly" poet was one who embraced Aestheticism, which was about Art for Art's sake and Beauty for Beauty's sake and, somewhere just below the surface, sex. I hadn't read the Aesthetic poets (Rossetti, Swinburne, Wilde), but I didn't have to. For Gilbert, Aestheticism was merely a pose, and his great charlatan Bun-thorne was brilliant at striking it:

> You must lie upon the daisies and discourse in novel
>   phrases of your complicated state of mind,
> The meaning doesn't matter if it's only idle chatter of a
>   transcendental kind.
> And ev'ry one will say,
> As you walk your mystic way,

"If this young man expresses himself in terms too deep
  for me,
Why, what a very singularly deep young man this deep
  young man must be!"

Everyone in *Patience* is striking some kind of pose, and
the characters all switch poses in midstream. That's why the
opera is such fun. But it's about a very specific British cultural
moment, and Richard D'Oyly Carte wanted to make sure
American audiences would understand what Gilbert was ridi-
culing. So he sent Oscar Wilde on a US lecture tour dressed
like Bunthorne: velvet smoking jacket, tight knee breeches,
silk stockings, patent leather opera pumps. The tactic worked,
and the American production was a success. Did Wilde even
realize he was being used as a marketing gambit? Or was he
having too good a time swanning around on D'Oyly Carte's
dime to care?

The contralto in *Patience*, Lady Jane, swoons over Bunthorne with the other rapturous maidens but is (of course)
considered ridiculous because she's older and stouter. I loved a
photo of Ann Drummond-Grant in that role, standing apart,
looking magnificently sad. It was probably her way of portray-
ing a rejected woman, but her expression haunted me. She
looked like someone who'd really lost something.

She didn't sing Lady Jane on my recording. I didn't allow
myself to wonder why, because I was determined to love all my
recordings equally. It was willful ignorance, and it couldn't last.

11

DEAR MISS MENTER

AUGUST 8, 1968, WAS MOTHER'S fifty-second birthday. I'd bought her an umbrella, since for some reason we didn't have any in the house. (In Syracuse, where it never stopped raining.) It was also the day Richard Nixon accepted the Republican nomination for president, and I knew enough to be alarmed that, with Bobby Kennedy gone, he had a good chance of winning. I mentioned these things in my notebook before getting to Ann Drummond-Grant. One of her recordings, *Princess Ida*, had been in my head since I heard it the day before, and it made me unreasoningly happy. I wrote, not for the first time: "Sometimes I think I will die of all this beauty."

When I got home from summer school, a blue air mail envelope from the Savoy Hotel was waiting for me. It contained the following letter, neatly typed on onionskin paper:

Dear Miss Menter,

Miss Bridget D'Oyly Carte was most interested to read your letter, and thanks you very much for writing to her, but has asked me to reply as she is about to go away for a few days holiday.

To begin with, it must be remembered that this is an English Company and therefore, if you were engaged to work for us in any capacity whatever, you would have to obtain a British Work Permit.

Secondly, while we should be very pleased to hear you sing at any time, we do not engage choristers under the age of eighteen, so I think the best thing would be for you to concentrate on having your voice properly trained; even people with the finest natural voices have to have good training, as irreparable damage could be done through incorrect breathing, bad production and so on. Then, if we are in New York during, say, 1970 or 1971, we could arrange to hear you sing at an audition there, or perhaps round about that time you yourself might be making a visit to this country when I am sure something could be arranged.

All this may sound rather depressing and far away, but the basis of a career as a professional singer is good, sound training.

I am sorry to tell you that Ann Drummond-Grant died in September 1959, shortly after leaving the Company, so recordings are all we have left of her voice.

Yours Sincerely,
Joan Robertson
Secretary to General Manager

An altogether kind and gracious letter, it now seems to me. Joan Robertson spoke the truth: the D'Oyly Carte was happy to audition singers at any time, in any town, but they had to be real singers and eligible to work in Britain. I have to smile at the note of motherly encouragement in paragraph four. But this encouragement did not register in 1968. All that registered, apart from the bit about the work permit, was the letter's last sentence, the death sentence—not just Ann Drummond-Grant's death, but also mine. That sentence destroyed an entire imagined world, slashed it away like a knife. The woman I had adored and idolized, who had been a living presence in my life while I discovered who I was and wanted to be, who had made the world tolerable and beautiful, had been dead since I was six. Had been dead the first time I heard her voice.

Clearly some part of me had suspected this. There was the matter of Gillian Knight suddenly occupying the contralto roles on my recordings (and singing them, it seemed to me, not nearly as beautifully). I hadn't wanted to think that Ann Drummond-Grant had left the company, let alone the physical world. Yet several months before, in English class, I'd written a short story about a girl who idolizes an opera singer without realizing the singer has died. The story's narrator knows it. I knew it. But I refused to acknowledge it. I needed her alive.

I needed to be able to dream about meeting her someday, about getting a letter in her handwriting, about hearing more of her living voice. Which could not *not* be living. I quickly wrote a reply to Miss Robertson, saying that Ann Drummond-Grant hadn't died and never would, not as long as there was someone to operate a record player and say, "This is beautiful." I was aware I sounded like the teenage girl I was, and also that while my bereavement was fresh, Miss Robertson's was nine years in the past. It was an odd feeling of displacement.

I had never experienced the death of someone I loved. Nor had I ever loved anyone so much, or felt, despite the lack of physical evidence, so loved in return. It was the largest thing that had ever happened to me. It may still be the largest. And I couldn't talk about it to anyone, couldn't cry in front of anyone. Certainly not my mother, whose birthday it was. Or my father or my friends. I said I didn't feel well and refused dinner. I told myself I wouldn't eat for three days. I also vowed never to swear again. That vow was broken almost immediately, but I tried to keep the one about not eating. I didn't want to feel like eating. When I woke the next morning and it was all still true, I kept thinking: This is *horrible*. It seemed the first time I knew what the word meant.

And where was she in all this? The thought of her hadn't left me; she was as present as ever. Such was the power of those grooves in vinyl, the power of that physical voice. But Ann Drummond-Grant could not remain a physical woman. She had to become a kind of goddess, sitting triumphant in the fast-moving clouds, watching over me.

12

PRINCESS IDA

MY FRIENDS COULD SEE I WAS BROKEN, or at least extremely brittle, though I wouldn't say why. I refused to eat for two days. On the third day, Robin's father took the two of us to the Otsego County fair. (I'd never heard of Otsego County, which wasn't far away.) He wouldn't hear any talk of fasting, so I ate—quite a lot—and enjoyed the day, though I felt strangely hollow and terribly lonely. Robin and I each spent a quarter on a grab-bag prize; mine was a big fake pearl on a chain. I still have it.

There were several reasons for my impulse to fast. The most obvious was to draw an invisible cloak of mourning about myself. I also wanted to punish my own flesh, of which there was too intractably much. Also, it dawned on me that the last opera I'd heard before getting my letter was *Princess Ida*, in which the contralto sings:

> Hunger, I beg to state,
> Is highly indelicate.
> This is a fact profoundly true,
> So learn your appetites to subdue!

She's made fun of in the next stanza, but I was in a mood to take her literally. Since nobody in my world knew the first thing about *Princess Ida*, it was an ideal place to seek refuge.

Princess Ida is based on *The Princess*, a long narrative poem by Tennyson which I have not to this day managed to read, because it's unreadable. Gilbert parodied the poem twice, first as a farce and then as a comic opera. Such parodies were mainstays of Victorian theater, and now that I think about it, they're not very far from the send-ups of movies and musicals I read in *Mad Magazine* as a child. That's the story of my cultural education: encountering the parody before the thing itself.

Princess Ida champions the education of women, a hot topic in 1884. She has established a women's college that no man is allowed to enter. Gilbert, of course, finds this preposterous:

> A Woman's college! maddest folly going!
> What can girls learn within its walls worth knowing?

Ida's ideals are so high she's almost completely humorless. But she has a love interest, a prince she was betrothed to as a baby. He sneaks onto the campus with two of his pals, disguised as women, to try to change her mind. Three men in drag and a killjoy of a princess—it really is a Victorian Marx Brothers movie.

The opera's dialogue, like Tennyson's poem, is blank verse and pretty stilted. But the musical numbers are marvelous. Sullivan's score is daring and strange, and Gilbert's lyrics are particularly trenchant. Never mind that he's skewering feminism, women's colleges, and Darwin's theory of evolution—he's doing it really well.

My recording, from 1954, was one of my favorites, even though Ann Drummond-Grant, in the contralto role of Lady Blanche, had little to sing, and the soprano singing Princess Ida was strident and frequently flat. I didn't know that Ann Drummond-Grant had once sung Ida, and that this firebrand role suited her down to the ground.

Soon after I got the fateful letter, I rode the bus downtown to the main library and started looking at microfilm of the *New York Times* for September 1959. I found a four-paragraph obituary datelined September 11. "Ann Drummond-Grant, contralto, died today," it began. "She was in her early fifties."

Yes, she died on September 11, and it became my personal day of remembrance and reflection. Until it became everyone else's.

The obit said she had been the D'Oyly Carte's principal contralto since 1951. It also said she'd joined the company as a chorister in 1933 and risen to the rank of principal *soprano*. After which she "was absent from the company to gain a variety of stage experience, including legitimate roles, musical comedy, and pantomime." Knowing nothing about British pantomime, which is sung and danced with raucous abandon, I pictured her in silent whiteface like Marcel Marceau. I thought she must be talented indeed.

Well, she was. Soprano and contralto roles in G&S are galaxies apart. The sopranos are either haughtily operatic or adorably saucy, but all are lively, desirable young ladies. The contraltos, as I've said, are older and larger and therefore *un*desirable, like their theatrical antecedents, pantomime dames, usually played by men in drag. Sullivan objected to Gilbert's cruel characterizations and gave the contraltos some of his most affecting music.

Ann Drummond-Grant was the only singer in D'Oyly Carte history to perform both soprano and contralto roles. Not to mention the mezzo-soprano soubrette roles she recorded but never performed. Wanting every last bit of her voice, I bought the 1950 version of *The Yeomen of the Guard*, the most serious-minded G&S opera, though I already owned a recording from the sixties. Ann Drummond-Grant sings the soubrette role of Phoebe, a young girl in love, and of course she sings it beautifully. I had to be much older before I realized that she sounds like someone with way too much emotional experience for the part. Even when she's trying to sound lighthearted, she is weighty of soul.

13

NOTTINGHAM

I WAS STILL IN MOURNING WHEN SCHOOL started in September, a secret, genteel grief I planned to carry with dignity. But in 1968, dignity was out of the question. There was certainly none to be had at Nottingham High. Walking into that school was a frying-pan-to-fire affair.

My brothers graduated from Nottingham in the early sixties, when it was an elite city school nestled in what some called the Tel Aviv Hills. (There were also Catholics and Protestants and Hindus, but any neighborhood with Jews in it became a Jewish neighborhood.) Nottingham students back then were white, clean-cut, and college bound. When I got there, the place was a war zone, and forced integration was the cause.

At the time, I couldn't process this. After three years in a junior high that had likewise been integrated by fiat, I was used to a certain amount of chaos. But I was also used to being with kids from different backgrounds and seeing all kinds of faces around me. I could feel that racial tensions were simmering. At Nottingham, they exploded.

Twenty years later, a sociologist named Gerald Grant wrote an entire book about what happened at Nottingham. I can boil it down to a paragraph: Black students were bused *en masse* to a white school where they were not welcomed. They were treated unfairly by white teachers—and students—who met them with suspicion, distrust, and worse. Discrimination had long been the way of things, but in 1968, the year Martin Luther King was murdered, it just wasn't acceptable anymore.

Before I'd been at the school a month, we had our first race riot, in the cafeteria. It was started by some of the bused-in Black kids. Chairs were thrown. One hit the principal in the head, cracking his skull. He bore the scar on his forehead for the rest of his tenure in the job and probably ever after.

According to Gerald Grant, it wasn't exactly true that the Black kids started the riot. They were reacting to what had happened a few nights before at a school dance, when white fraternity kids told them to "Get out of our school!" I might have thrown a chair at someone who said that to me.

That first riot was the beginning of the end of the old order, the beginning of a movement toward coexistence. But it didn't happen fast, and my years at Nottingham were the most violent. There were further riots, and threats of riots—almost as bad because of the fear in the air and the constant police presence. There were turf wars in the corridors; instead of student hall monitors, we had paid security guards and a cop. The principal hired at the beginning of my senior year—his predecessor having resigned, exhausted—regularly confiscated knives, clubs, chains, and lead pipes. When his life was threatened, he was assigned a bodyguard.

Those were gentler times. Today there would be guns.

I don't remember discussing any of this with my parents, and I don't recall them attending the parent–teacher meetings that tried to address the situation. I was basically on my own, scuttling from one class to the next and more than occasionally being shut inside a classroom while chaos raged in the halls. The bell would sound three times, a signal that all hell was breaking loose, and the teachers were to lock their doors.

I remember one such incident in my junior year when my

Latin teacher, the magnificent Carmelia Metosh, shut the door and said in her booming voice, "Remember—they have to go through me to get to you!" She was a formidable woman, and I didn't doubt that she meant it. She continued the lesson.

She was tougher than some of her colleagues. My high school yearbook is dedicated to an English teacher who was assaulted in the girls' lavatory and left crippled and bedridden. A favorite history teacher got his leg broken in a riot and taught for the rest of the year in a wheelchair. By the time I graduated in 1971, nearly three-quarters of the teachers who'd been at Nottingham in 1966 had left the school. It would take another decade to establish something like harmony between whites and Blacks, during which time many white families moved to the suburbs.

And yet. Scary as those years were, there was an enormous sense of liberation. Nobody wanted those old rules back. Fraternities, sororities, proms—we thought we were abolishing them for good. Our 1971 yearbook is unlike any that came before it: more creative, more playful, more politically aware. There's a (staged) full-page photo of a female student threatening the principal with a plastic assault rifle, and a board game where you can land on spaces saying: "1st Riot: play catch with chairs in the cafeteria" or "Window broken: librarian turns into toad." There are as many Black faces as white in the candid photos. Faces of kids I knew and liked.

Most of the Black kids at Nottingham had nothing to do with the riots; they just surfed the violence like the rest of us. They were awakening to their cultural identities and infusing the school with new energy. I remember a performance by a dance–theater group called The Soul Generation that had the auditorium on its feet. The power of movement, the power of the voices—this was Black Power that spoke to us all.

How can I be sorry about an education like this? Proms

and sororities, those trumped-up things, would have been torture for me. I was glad not to have to pretend to care, or not care, about them. The war in Vietnam was raging. Nixon, the new president, was lying about it. Boys in my class could be drafted at eighteen. I realized that my class had a responsibility to speak out, or at least to know what was going on.

I haven't mentioned the drugs, of which there were a lot. Unlike most of my friends, I never smoked pot. I toyed with the idea of trying it, but worried that I'd lose control and start babbling about Ann Drummond-Grant. She was that close to the surface.

But we all started dressing more like hippies, which basically meant being more bohemian and less clean-cut: Afros for the Black kids, Jew-fros for the nerdy white boys, long straight hair for the rest of us (male and female). Girls were finally allowed to wear pants to school, and some of us showed up in long Earth-mother skirts. I found the nerve to jettison the horrid little panty girdle my mother thought I should wear. And along with Gilbert and Sullivan, I now had all the songs from *Hair* running through my head:

> Black boys are nutritious
> Black boys fill me up
> Black boys are so damn yummy
> They satisfy my tummy
> I have such a sweet tooth when it comes to love . . .

14

MISS RIGSBEE

MIND YOU, I HADN'T YET kissed any boy, Black or white. To discourage anyone who might have considered kissing me, I became the smart aleck in the room, acting like it was my job to be clever. I did this even in my own head, curating my thoughts like someone was listening. When I spoke in class, I edited the words as they came out of my mouth, conscious of timing and delivery. One of the boys regularly became part of my act by interpolating: "Marcia! Shut up!" (He wrote it in my yearbook. I took it for affection.) It was a fine smokescreen for a girl in love with a dead singer. That love was an identity, a vine I could grasp to swing through life.

Race riots couldn't touch me. Striding through long institutional halls that rang with clanging voices, clanging bells, clanging locker doors—the place looked like it was built to be flushed with a fire hose—I was the girl who was going to be a singer, whatever it took.

The music classrooms had a wing of their own. This was for soundproofing but had the added benefit of setting them apart from the chaos. Early on, I found a haven in the choir room where Elisabeth Rigsbee taught. She was an odd duck, but she was the duck I needed.

The room was built like an amphitheater, with six tiers of seats rising to venetian-blinded windows at the back. I'm sure it could have sat a hundred; that first day of choir there were at least thirty of us. From my perch in the third or fourth row, I looked down at Miss Rigsbee, a slim blonde woman in her midforties.

In a clear voice that was precise to the point of prissiness, she told us we were going to sing Nottingham's Alma Mater and handed out a mimeographed sheet with the words. Then she sang it for us in her trained soprano, enunciating prissily:

Nottingham, Nottingham, faithful and true,
Alma Mater, we're loyal to you,
We will sing thy praise in glory all our days,
Thee we will remember in our hearts forever. . . .

I could already see that Nottingham was no longer that sort of alma mater, and that for most of its students, Miss Rigsbee's performance would be something to titter at. But I wanted to answer her good diction with some of my own. In a D'Oyly Carte chorus, every word was enunciated crisply and in perfect unison. A *t* at the end of a word shot forth like a whipcrack. Miss Rigsbee's precision felt like home.

I was determined to shine for her even more when she asked a senior named Elvira to take the last lines as a solo.

Memories, memories, our thoughts of old
Happy hours of yesterday unfold.

I thought, *I should be singing those lines. Ann Drummond-Grant sings the word memories in* The Sorcerer, *and memorials in* Iolanthe. *I want to sing it like she does, slowly and ruefully.* I thought, *Elvira's the best she's got? I can do better.*

From that first day, Miss Rigsbee became a friend and mentor to me. A few of the boys would sing *Eleanor Rigby* under their breaths when she walked into the classroom, because she wasn't married and looked to them like someone who was lonely, or maybe because the similar names made it irresistible. Or because she was so unfailingly prim. Except she wasn't, really. She was disciplined and rigorous. To me, she was what a serious musician looked like.

Did I tell her about Ann Drummond-Grant? Absolutely not.

I loved choir because I thought I had the best voice in the soprano section. It was true I sang on pitch, and my high notes rang out brilliantly. I could read music, more or less, and was deeply interested in getting my part right. But the voice—at a certain age, singers start referring to "the voice" rather than "my voice"—the voice was young and slender. Clear and true at the top, breathy at the middle, nonexistent at the bottom. A girl's lyric soprano.

It wasn't fair, to my mind, that someone built like me—wide hipped, broad shouldered, extravagantly fleshed (the wobbly thighs and upper arms, the C-cup breasts, the ineradicable pot belly)—should have such a little silver bell of a voice. So I decided it was bigger than it was, which was easy because I never listened to recordings of it. It sounded big in my own head. I figured I could be the star of any choir. But I couldn't get into all of them, and there were a fair number to audition for.

All City Choir was a slam dunk. Miss Rigsbee coached me for All County, which accepted me that first year, and All State, which didn't. The auditions were supposed to be good experience, but I saw them as hurdles to jump, ways to prove to myself that I was already a star. As I wrote again and again in my notebook, I needed to be stellar if I was going to be a D'Oyly Carte chorister.

Two other teachers were important to me. One was the redoubtable Latin teacher, Mrs. Metosh, who spoke loudly and wore a loud but not unpleasing fragrance. When I asked what it was, she said, "Estée Lauder bath oil," by which I soon realized she meant Youth Dew. I wouldn't have admitted to wearing a fragrance called Youth Dew either. She was in her fifties, heavyset and heavily rouged, with a stern dark-eyed face like the mosaic portrait of the Pompeian matron in the Museo de Capodimonte in Naples. (Her maiden name was Monaco.) She always wore sleeveless dresses, a fashion choice I understand only now, from the far side of menopause.

Latin was all rules and memorization, and Mrs. Metosh was rigorous. But she made rigor more entertaining than any of my teachers before or since. As she exhorted us to admire Julius Caesar's crisp sentences, she gossiped about him wickedly, which is always appropriate with the Romans. "It was said that even in the provinces, no woman was safe from Caesar," she told us, quoting Suetonius's quip that Caesar was "every woman's man and every man's woman." Once she figured we'd been given enough to memorize for the day, she'd just sit and talk to us—about Rome, about her daughter's Siamese cat that craved ladyfingers, about trying to drive up the treacherous hill on West Seneca Turnpike behind some idiot (or *dingle*, her term of choice) who didn't know how to drive in snow. We listened raptly. We called her Regina or, more often, Queen.

French class brought a different sort of rapture. I instantly developed a humiliating crush on the young teacher, who was not—*not!*—attractive but threw some unknown switch in me, spurring a frantic, tongue-tied obsessiveness I couldn't write about, let alone talk about. He was handsome in a sweaty, moon-faced way and tried to act cool in a manner that guaranteed he never would be. He spoke French with a strong Syracuse accent (notably the flat *a*, where "flat" is pronounced "*flee*-uht"). How could I have a crush on such a buffoon? What was the nature of this crush that hijacked my body and mortified my mind? I didn't want to know.

In other classes I fidgeted, passed notes, daydreamed, not learning much and not caring. I'd taken a subscription to *The New York Times*, but the inky papers piled up at the bottom of my locker, unread except for the tiny classified ads that said the D'Oyly Carte Company was coming in November. I lived for that.

15

A BAD COUGH

MY FATHER AND I WERE NOT in the habit of taking father–daughter trips. As a small child, I'd spent a lot of time in his car while he made house calls, looking at some snowbank while he went inside to tend to the patient. He drove me to nursery school and Sunday school. He'd ask me, "What are you thinking about so hard?" And I'd prattle away. I loved my Daddy then and tried to be smart for him. But he was elusive. I could rarely charm him into reading bedtime stories because something else claimed his attention. He worked day and night; he catnapped and couldn't be disturbed; he went out somewhere with Mother, who also felt starved for his attention. He wasn't a cuddler, but he sometimes let me sit in his lap, which was more than Mother did.

By the time I was a teenager, I'd learned to guard the things I loved, because all adolescents do this and because I sensed my father's predatory interest in my emotional life. He fed on my enthusiasms for performers and music and words; my open feelings had to carry the weight of his closed-off ones. I didn't put it in those terms. I just felt uncomfortable with him, even though I still adored him.

Our trip to New York was a balancing act. I needed to be overtly grateful for the enormous treat of seeing the D'Oyly Carte, but I also needed to protect my emotional real estate, the sacred space where I worshipped Ann Drummond-Grant. So I never mentioned her, though I carried her name in my mouth and looked for her on every street corner, as if she were still traveling with the company and I might catch a glimpse of her.

And of course, being a young lady and no longer a child, I had to act poised and confident, as though I'd come into possession of a womanly beauty that had yet to manifest. My father acted like he thought I was beautiful, and sometimes I could almost go along with it. But when he took me to dinner in a New York restaurant so fancy it had a dessert cart, and then made a pun about the doily on the cart, I only felt flustered and ungainly, in addition to being properly annoyed by the wordplay.

I wasn't ready to pretend I was a woman. The unflattering dresses my mother bought me, the pantyhose, the short haircut with bangs, supposedly made more sophisticated by the addition of a little height from a roller set at the top: I felt like I had a tiny head on top of a huge body, and the rabbit-fur coat didn't help. It was thick and boxy and made me look enormous. Besides being too warm for November.

But we were in New York! Which I'd only visited once before, at age ten, when we had put my brother Robert on a boat for his pre-college summer trip to Europe. (Both my brothers got to travel on a Eurail Pass for a month when they graduated from high school. This wasn't offered to me.) Manhattan was as I remembered it, exhausting and overwhelming, dirty and exhilarating. We kept to one small part of Midtown, near City Center on West 55th Street, where the D'Oyly Carte was in residence.

We saw *Iolanthe* and *The Mikado* in successive performances; one must have been a matinee, but I don't remember. I've blotted it out. I didn't write it down. What I remember, aside from my giddy nervousness at seeing my "friends" onstage and the pleasant surprise of finding the dialogue genuinely funny, was that I went backstage after *The Mikado* and staged a coughing fit. It started out as a fake fit and became a real one. I coughed until there were tears in my eyes, standing next to a piece of scenery I recognized from *Patience*, part of a set Ann Drummond-Grant must have touched. People were very solicitous. Someone brought me water.

I'd read somewhere about a young woman staging a coughing fit to get noticed. It seemed a properly theatrical gambit for a girl with theatrical ambitions. I was sure nobody would talk to me if I simply presented myself—though in reality, D'Oyly Carte principals went out of their way to acknowledge the fans who sent them flowers or waited for autographs at the stage door. They were grateful, hard-working folk. But I was too shy and tongue-tied to think of anything to do but cough. An awkward girl in a big coat. Or perhaps my father carried the coat.

My father told me afterward, in a matter-of-fact tone designed to convey a lesson, that while I was coughing, he'd been having a chat with the Mikado. I could have killed him. The Mikado was Donald Adams, the bass baritone who sang the role on my recording and was a hero of mine. But they were all my heroes.

Once the fit subsided, I did get to talk to some of them: John Reed, the comic baritone who actually laughed at my impersonation of a Syracuse accent. Kenneth Sandford, who sang Pooh-Bah and the other heavy baritone roles. Phillip Potter, the melodious tenor who was so handsome I couldn't put two coherent words together. And Christene Palmer, the contralto who didn't stand a chance in my estimation, though she was perfectly fine.

I didn't mention Ann Drummond-Grant to any of them. I couldn't bring myself to speak her name, though I was desperate to know about her. What was she like? Was she wonderful? How could she *not* have been wonderful?

At the end, I had a moment with Donald Adams, who said (twice!) in his magnificent gruff voice, "I wish you every success." I'm sure he meant it. I wished it too. Wishing was all I understood. Watching the performers leave the theater in their street clothes, I was sure that light surrounded them wherever they went, that they existed on a higher plane than I knew how to reach.

16

THE WE OF ME

I CONSIDERED THE D'OYLY CARTE to be my true family, "the
we of me," as Carson McCullers put it in *The Member of the
Wedding*. I'd seen the film of that novel and loved Julie Harris's
portrayal of a tomboy longing to belong to something. For all
my mooning about wanting to sing and act, I don't believe I
ever really wanted to be a star with fans waiting at a stage door.
I just wanted to be among the we of me, the people who considered me normal and not weird or affected.

I *was* affected. People thought I spoke with a British accent,
and I would have if I could've gotten away with it. It certainly
wasn't a Syracuse accent. It was a clear, non-regional American accent, almost but not quite as prim as Miss Rigsbee's. I
spoke as if Gilbert himself were listening, in clearly enunciated
convoluted sentences, never using a small word where a larger
one would do. My friends made fun of these sesquipedalian
proclivities, but they liked it best when I applied my incisive
diction to four-letter words: "You sound so sophisticated when
you swear!"

When I got home from New York, I wrote Bridget D'Oyly
Carte to tell her I had swooned in the presence of Philip Potter
and made John Reed laugh. I didn't mention the coughing fit.
She sent me a Christmas card with her florid signature. It had
a colorful illustration of G&S characters on a little stage, with

Iolanthe flying overhead trailing a banner that said, "AMERI-CAN TOUR 1968–9." Inside was a typed message:

> Thank you so much for your amusing letter; I am so glad you enjoyed the two Operas in New York and that you were able to speak to some of the members of the Company.

From then on, I was on the D'Oyly Carte mailing list. They sent me notices of tour dates in cities all over England: Black-pool, Harrogate, Sheffield, Bradford, Manchester, Hull. All I saw were names of places I was not going to get to. I never thought about how much work this schedule meant for every-one involved, from Miss Carte on down. The D'Oyly Carte was a touring company, on the road forty-eight weeks a year, with eight performances per week, plus rehearsals. Except for the London season, they didn't perform the same opera twice in succession—which meant that the sets they traveled with were constantly being struck and rebuilt. Costumes had to be pressed and wigs dressed for every performance. Understudies had to be rehearsed and ready to step in on short notice. Every member of the company felt responsible for producing a tight, polished performance, come what may, time after time. They were bonded to each other like soldiers on an endless cam-paign—and it was endless, considering that the D'Oyly Carte had been touring since 1878.

I had some inkling of this from the books I'd read, partic-ularly *Martyn Green's Treasury of Gilbert and Sullivan*. Martyn Green was the famous comic baritone on my 1951 recordings, the ones with Ann Drummond-Grant in the soubrette roles. He had joined the company in 1922 and understudied Henry Lytton, who had learned the roles in Gilbert's time. I knew his voice well: it was not large but supple. He was comfortable with the recording process and, unlike some of his colleagues, sang into the microphone in an intimate way rather than projecting as he would in a theater.

Green's writing also had a certain intimacy, as though he were talking to me over a glass of Scotch, of which he was extremely fond. The *Treasury* basically consists of the librettos of the operas with his annotations. He explains hundreds of obscure Victorian references, talks about performance practices, and gossips about things that went wrong. Like the time the contralto playing Lady Jane in *Patience* swept onstage without realizing that a large corset, draped on a chair in her dressing room, had somehow attached itself to the back of her costume. Hearing titters from the chorus, she wheeled around to face them, hissing, "What is so damn funny?" to huge audience laughter.

This must have happened in the thirties, but it made me laugh as if I'd been—not in that audience, but onstage with my compatriots, the ladies of the chorus. Thanks to the spate of D'Oyly Carte memoirs published in recent years, I know that Ann Drummond-Grant had a similar underwear mishap in the fifties. Playing the Fairy Queen in *Iolanthe*, she came onstage for her big second-act number with a large brassiere dangling from one of her wings. She wasn't aware of it, and the audience never saw it, because the choristers managed to squelch their laughter, snatch the bra and pass it, fairy to fairy, offstage. But that's a story about a human woman. It would have embarrassed me at fifteen, when I needed to see her as a goddess.

There was another library book I borrowed and re-borrowed in those days: *A Picture History of Gilbert and Sullivan*, filled with black-and-white photos of D'Oyly Carte productions from Gilbert's day to the early sixties. I learned the names of all the players, the costumes they wore, and the sets they traveled with. There were several shots of Ann Drummond-Grant onstage. The images were tiny, but I could admire her regal stance as the Duchess of Plaza Toro and her fine sadness as Lady Jane. Those photos were my icons, instruments of presence and mystery. Words uttered before them might be heard.

Wanting to own these images, I began to copy them in charcoal pencil on a large drawing pad. There was the head shot that had accompanied one of her obituaries, as Katisha, mouth corners turned imperiously down. There was Lady Jane, rejected and abandoned. The Fairy Queen, smiling beneficently, sketched from a library copy of *Theatre Arts* magazine. And two photos from a book Miss Rigsbee lent me: one of Little Buttercup in mid-song, which I couldn't get right. (The mouth looked tortured.) And a photo from the 1955 American tour. She's with other cast members, newly arrived in San Francisco. They're waving; the sun is on their faces. The image is unclear, but I can see the suit jacket and blouse that was a kind of offstage uniform for her. And the hat, of course. All the women wore hats.

My drawings were not good. (No one ever saw them.) I learned that when you copy something from a photo, it looks twice as flat and static unless you really know how to draw. But reproducing those images, however clumsily, was a way of being present with her, as one might copy a poem in order to get inside it. I had nothing else of her Lady Jane or her Fairy Queen because she never recorded those roles. I expended a lot of energy wishing I could go back in time and hear her perform. I still believe it's possible, or will be after I die, given that time itself is an illusion.

17

VIRGINITY

I WROTE DISAPPROVINGLY IN MY NOTEBOOK that my friend Anne had become a hippie, skipping half days of school and even—once— trying pot. She must have been bored out of her mind at Nottingham. Nobody, least of all her parents, noticed her absences; she did fine on her exams and graduated a year early. She was in the vanguard. By senior year, quite a few of us weren't bothering to attend the classes that bored us, especially gym. Skipping gym was supposed to disqualify us from graduating, but it didn't—they would have had to hold back a third of the senior class.

What alarmed me most about Anne was that she seemed to want to lose her virginity. She was in the vanguard there too, but not by much. At sixteen and seventeen, most of my friends were circling the idea of sex and some of them actually had it. It seemed to me they were popping off one by one. *Pop, pop, pop.* They had sex because they had serious boyfriends or just wanted to get it over with. They must have had birth control, too, or luck, because nobody I knew got pregnant. As for me, I pinned my formless longings on unavailable older men, the more unavailable the better. Boys my own age seemed immature, like pre-men, perhaps because the men in my family were so much older.

There was another, half-conscious reason I was squeamish about sex. When I was two or three years old, one of my brother

Julian's friends, a boy of fifteen, came into my room, got into my bed and made me hold his penis. I hadn't known there was such a thing. It was huge, pulsing—I could barely get my tiny hands around it—and unpleasantly moist, almost waxy. I was terrified, and very aware that Julian, my alleged babysitter, was downstairs, failing to intervene.

As a toddler, I had no frame of reference for this sexual assault. As a grownup, I tried to downplay it by telling myself it happened only once. But I never forgot it or told anyone. (Of course he'd told me not to tell.) I did occasionally think I'd like to ask him to let me hold it again and see what I'd do to it this time. But he's old now. Maybe he's dead. Either way, his manhood lives only in memory.

This may explain why I felt that sex was something enormous, something I wasn't remotely ready for; and why I dreamed of holy love, capital-L Love, the kind I had for my operas. I couldn't imagine sharing that love with some sweaty boy. The closer I came to feeling physical desire, the more I fled to G&S, where a fairy was a magical winged being and not another word for homosexual, and where all young ladies had intact hymens (surely!) under their crinolines. I was as Victorian as I could contrive to be, unaware that the Victorian Age had a spectacularly raunchy side.

I practiced the piano. I prepared for choral auditions. Miss Rigsbee invited me to join a chamber choir and gave me a solo. I was sure I was on my way. But Miss Pinnell was still not ready to entertain the idea of teaching me.

I wrote another letter to Joan Robertson on Savoy Hill, asking her to tell me more about Ann Drummond-Grant, including whether she'd worn a ring on the middle finger of her right hand—I thought I could discern one in that San Francisco photo.

"Ann Drummond-Grant was a very wonderful person and one whom I am proud to have known," she wrote back. There followed a CV of her time with the company: She joined as a soprano chorister in 1933, was understudying principal roles by 1935, and became a principal soprano in 1937. Not an unusual progression; quite a few D'Oyly Carte principals rose from the chorus. But she wasn't a principal for long. In December 1938, she "left to do other work such as musical comedy, pantomime, summer shows, etc."

And then: "During the next years, while she was doing this sort of work, her voice deepened, as is so often the case, with the result that in August 1950, Miss Drummond-Grant came back to the Company as its principal contralto. . . ." Wait a minute. How often is this actually the case? Mostly it isn't. Sopranos do not become contraltos. But a large soprano voice can settle into its true identity in a lower register, as a mezzo-soprano. Big voices take a long time to mature.

Then, something I hadn't known: "She was married to Isidore Godfrey, then our musical director, and they had no children. He has subsequently married again and is now retired. I am afraid I do not know whether Miss Drummond-Grant wore any rings apart from her wedding ring."

She was married! This was world-changing news. It meant . . . it meant she'd had sex, which I was planning never to do because I couldn't face the thought of it. And because I believed I'd never want anyone who would want me. But if *she* could marry . . .

I began to replan my life.

Joan Robertson's letter left out certain key facts I learned many years later. Miss Drummond-Grant was already seeing her future husband, the musical director, while she was rising through the ranks as a soprano, and he was married to someone else. Company management, terrified that this would create a scandal, phased her out of the principal roles she'd worked so hard to win.

The D'Oyly Carte had been obsessed with propriety since its early days when theater was not respectable. Even in 1938, Miss Drummond-Grant's behavior would have been scandalous. In her hometown of Edinburgh, she'd have been pilloried. But what an un-hussy-like woman she was! A tall, serious-minded spinster in her thirties, a good daughter from a proper Scottish home, a church soloist who'd arguably been drawn to the company because it was respectable.

I myself became involved with a married man and eventually married him, one day before what would have been her forty-fourth wedding anniversary. But I'm getting ahead of my story.

18

ALONE,
AND YET ALIVE

JANUARY 1969. MARTIN LUTHER KING's birthday marked for the first time since his murder. Long nights, bleak days, snow and the detritus of snow. Though there is a sense of a new thin light coming into the world in a Syracuse January, it's a light sitting atop boundless darkness, with the worst of winter yet to come. A thaw means slush, and the slush is dirty. The place for winter festivals is in the mind, where the light is brightest. At least that's how it was for me.

Gilbert and Sullivan is happy and brilliantly lit, all of it, even the serious parts. When I listened to the operas, as much in my head as on vinyl, the sound was ablaze with color, alive with rhythm; the lyrics thrummed with a benign, exalted cleverness. The operas welcomed me warmly. They were home, more than the physical home through which I moved nervously and furtively, afraid to do anything to make my mother speak sharply, though sharply was how she spoke. There was no pleasing Mother—by which I mean not that she was displeased with me but that she seemed to take little pleasure in life. I could find no secret doorway to the things that made her happy. So I went through my own doorway to where the music was.

Each opera had a different sound palette. *The Mikado*, my first opera, seemed the richest and brightest. It was home to

Katisha and her glorious expressions of sorrow amid the general silliness. In Act II, right after "The flowers that bloom in the spring," a romp of a trio for the soprano, tenor, and comic baritone, Katisha, the rejected woman, comes onstage alone and sings about wanting to die.

> Alone, and yet alive! Oh, sepulchre!
> My soul is still my body's prisoner!
> Remote the peace that death alone can give—
> My doom, to wait! My punishment, to live!

I didn't know what a sepulchre was, though I thought it a fine dark word. Sullivan—subverting Gilbert's meter, as usual—sets these pentameter lines as a slow recitative, with the words "to wait" on a shining high note, and "to live" landing an octave and a half lower. A plunge into darkness. Then:

> Hearts do not break!
> They sting and ache
> For old love's sake,
> But do not die,
> Though with each breath
> They long for death
> As witnesseth
> The living I!

[Witnesseth? That's there for the rhyme scheme. "As witness," a legal term. Gilbert was a barrister.]

> Oh, living I!
> Come, tell me why,
> When hope is gone,
> Dost thou stay on?
> [. . .]
> May not a cheated maiden die?

These short, repetitive, nursery-rhymed lines are Gilbert getting out of Sullivan's way, providing a spare framework for a soaring aria. And soar it does, from a climactic high F above treble C ("when hope is gone") down to a low B-flat (on "cheated"). A real contralto can stop the show here. In the next scene, Katisha is asked to be very silly indeed, but in this one she's dead serious, and Ann Drummond-Grant sang it like she meant it. It seemed to me that she pleaded too hard to die, and that someone granted her wish. She did tend to see the dark side of things. She was, according to those who knew her, wreathed in habitual Scottish gloom. But it must have brought her enormous pleasure to sing this number as well as she did.

The thing is, Katisha doesn't die. She allows herself to be wooed by Ko-Ko, the comic baritone (whom she calls "this miserable object") because she's no longer young and is running out of time. "I am an acquired taste," she cries. "It takes *years* to train a man to love me." Katisha, strong and imperious, prime mover of the plot, keeps insisting she's alive. Ann Drummond-Grant was anything but, and that put her into a strange new space, a bardo—in Tibetan Buddhism, the existence between one lifetime and the next. Her recorded voice, for me, remained persistently alive. I couldn't have a personal relationship with her, but I could feel her presence in my own being, behind that inner door. She watched over me, though not in the peeping-tom way that God was supposed to watch over people. She was simply there, and she was there for me.

I'd been in love with her, with the idea of her, with her living voice—the living I. Now it was difficult to sustain that intensity of in-love-ness, which lost its source of oxygen when I learned of her death. But I found that the dead have one large advantage over the living. They never let you down.

19

HANS CONRIED, MARTYN GREEN, AND THE DRAGON LADY

Though I would have denied it, my parents were paying attention to who I was and what I wanted to become. One of them—which?—suggested I spend the summer of 1969 as an apprentice at the local summer theater. I had no idea what this entailed but liked the idea. It fitted my master plan.

Is there even such a thing as summer stock anymore? It certainly doesn't exist as it did then, when shows traveled from place to place on what was called the Straw Hat Circuit. The performers were a mix of hopefuls on their way up, stars on their way down, and journeyman actors somewhere in the middle. We got the guy who *sounded* like Robert Goulet.

Costumes traveled with the actors, but the sets, lights, props, and pit orchestra (for musicals) were furnished by the local venues. These were professional shows staffed by union members. We apprentices were unpaid grunts who built the shows by day and worked backstage by night. It was glorious. The less sleep we got, the gloriouser it was. Our theater was in a high school on the North Side, another windowless building where you could lose all sense of time. Mother ferried me there. At sixteen, I was old enough to drive but had no desire to learn.

The other apprenti (as we called ourselves, with a long *i*) came from all over town—nice kids, not all of whom aspired to perform. Performing was the least of it. By the time the actors trooped in to begin their one-week run, sets had been built, lights had been hung, props had been gathered, and there was a book-length list of cues (lights, sound, props, flies, curtains) in the hands of the stage manager who had to make everything work. At the end of the week, the old show was struck and the new one went up, in the space of a day. It was my idea of heaven—not so much the endless work as the fervor attached to it.

The sets were flimsy by design, canvas flats that could be pried apart as quickly as they'd been nailed together. From the house, they looked solid and real. I was amazed that, with very little tutelage, I could build a flat, cover it with canvas, and, once it was painted to look like wallpaper or whatever, spatter it with black to make the image appear three dimensional.

I wanted to get close to the performers, to enter their world. I watched them, interacted with them, without really understanding the relentless ambition of the younger actors or the dogged professionalism of the older ones. The young ones had been performing since they were kids and were already members of Actors' Equity. They had trained voices like buzz saws and could tap-dance like pros. They *were* pros. Never did it occur to me that if I wanted to do anything like what they were doing, I was way behind in my training.

The older actors were a pleasure to watch. Offstage, they paced themselves, snatching every bit of rest they could. Onstage, they gave the audience their money's worth. Ray Bolger, touring at age sixty-five in a sodden musical called *The Happy Time*, high-kicked his way down a ladder in a song-and-dance number, belting out the lyrics with energy to spare.

That was the last show of the summer. The first was a comedy called *Spofford* that had just closed on Broadway. (All our shows had closed.) It concerned a Connecticut chicken farmer who has an existential crisis while hobnobbing with New York weekenders and a priapic poet called Gowan McGland, a sit-com version of Dylan Thomas. More than this you do not need to know. Our chicken farmer was Hans Conried, an actor I knew from the many TV comedies where he had played someone ethnic or an egghead or an ethnic egghead. He was tall and lanky, with a repertoire of sneers and a penetrating voice that was deployed to advantage in the more intelligent cartoons.

I had a thing for Hans Conried. Not just because he was so familiar, but because I sensed he really was as erudite and thoughtful as he sounded and might thus be sympathetic to a teenage girl who had all of Gilbert and Sullivan by heart. So I was thrilled to learn, on the day we were decapitating dozens of rubber chickens to use as props, that I had been assigned to be his dresser.

I did not actually dress Hans Conried. I had to iron his slouchy linen jacket and hand it to him from the wings during the show, along with sundry objects including a can of beer, which I was instructed to shake so it would spray when he opened it. (They were going for every laugh they could get.) There wasn't much else. He took care of his own clothes and wore little or no makeup—he could pass for a craggy old chicken farmer without help, though he was only fifty-two. His maxim was "Never stand when you can sit, and never sit when you can lie down." Onstage, he was focused and energetic, keenly aware of the need to keep the wan little play moving. Every night after the first act, he asked the stage manager what the timing had been. Shorter was better.

I heard him say that a career in show business was a beggar's life, but I could see he loved his work. I was worshipfully attentive, banking his dressing room with wildflowers to the point where he said, "It looks like a mafia *funeral* in here." He, in turn, treated me with a quizzical affection. He called me Crazy Lady but said it tenderly. I didn't know it, but he had a daughter about my age.

I felt comfortable enough with him to banter about G&S, which, as I expected, he could quote prolifically. He told me he knew Martyn Green, one of my D'Oyly Carte idols, and that Green had called Bridget D'Oyly Carte a "dragon lady." I assured him this was not the case.

Actually, quite a few people thought Bridget D'Oyly Carte was a dragon lady. Her management style was remote and imperial. Green had left the company—along with two dozen other people—because he didn't like the way she ran it.

Miss Bridget was something of an autocrat and more than a bit of a snob. But she was also extremely shy, almost reclusive, the temperamental opposite of her impresario grandfather. At times she seemed more interested in sets and costumes than the people occupying them, though she actually cared about people, especially children, quite a lot. She had inherited a large share of the Savoy Hotel Group, of which she was vice-chairman, and the opera company, which she headed. She worked tirelessly at both jobs, chain-smoked like a demon, drank a lot of good Scotch whisky by herself, and kept a very low profile for someone who moved in high society. I had no idea how wealthy she was. All I knew was that she sent me Christmas cards. I was on her side. Whereas I'd written to Martyn Green earlier that year and was still unhappy with his reply.

Green was living in the US and working on Broadway, where I tracked him down. I sent him the usual letter about my aspirations, and he was—I now see—wonderfully honest with me.

As regards your life's ambition—that is, to be a member of the D'Oyly Carte Opera Company—during my association with them, it was never their policy to engage anyone who was not British, which of course included Australian, Canadian, etc., but not American. I do not know if they have changed their policy since that time, but quite candidly, I doubt it. There are, however, many small companies performing Gilbert and Sullivan in this country, all of whom, though not the D'Oyly Carte, give some excellent training and most creditable performances. I wish I could be more encouraging and helpful in your ambition, but this is the best I can do.

Should you ever see my name as being present and/ or performing anywhere that you might be able to come and see whatever show I am with, please send your name in, and I will try and give you some further encouragement.

Yours very truly,
MARTYN GREEN

I didn't want to hear any of this, especially the part about the many small companies offering excellent training. That sounded like penny-ante stuff to me. I was aiming for the top, and Miss Bridget hadn't said anything about Americans not being allowed. Martyn Green, the generous old pro, was telling me how it really was. I didn't believe him.

I might have emerged from my theatrical summer with a determination to work harder toward my goal—if I'd known what it meant to work. Hans Conried had performed Shakespeare in college and was an established character actor by his early twenties, mastering the very different techniques for stage, film, and radio. By the time I met him, he seemed to just walk onstage and perform. I imagined I would do that someday, somehow.

But my dream of performing was based in the past, not the future. No matter what I told myself, what I really wanted was to sing with the D'Oyly Carte in the 1950s, alongside people who were scattered or dead. I wanted to walk into my recordings and have my career there. Singing and acting were things that happened in my imagination, where I was free and happy. In my physical body—where performing actually happens—I was neither free nor happy nor comfortable being looked at.

20

VOICE LESSONS

But now, at sixteen, I was finally old enough to study with Ruth Pinnell. She had to accept me. She'd said she would. Vocal training was the key to every door that mattered, and Miss Pinnell was its keeper.

When I broached her studio on the Hill this time, she met me more with cordiality than enthusiasm. She ran me through some scales and gave me a list of music to buy, albums of arias and art songs for young voices. I figured that if they were right for my voice, I ought to be able to sing them right off the bat. At this point, I still believed I could sing.

The songs were in Italian. I didn't know any Italian, though I figured my passing familiarity with Latin would give me the gist. Besides, I had a good ear for languages. I'd pick it up.

But the first song I worked on was a mouthful and a puzzlement. It was said to be Mozart but was actually by someone named Mysliveček. The words went like this:

> *Ridente la calma nell'alma si desti;*
> *Né resti più segno di sdegno e timor.*
> *Tu vieni, frattanto, a stringer mio bene,*
> *Le dolce catene sí grate al mio cor.*

There was no translation, and back then, I couldn't Google it. I knew *calma* meant calm and *timor* meant fear and *mio cor* meant my heart, but that was as far as I got. I had the sense it didn't matter what the words meant, and indeed, they're generic as such lyrics go: "May a laughing calmness awaken in my soul; nor may there remain a trace of anger or fear. You are coming, my love, to tighten the sweet chains my heart is so grateful for." (Chains. My baby's got me locked up in chains.)

This aria is supposed to be a good teaching piece. It has a slow, sustained vocal line that encourages proper placement of the voice. I can even tell you what that sentence means.

The human voice is a wind instrument. Air—exhaled breath—passes through the larynx, which contains a pair of reeds: the vocal folds, or vocal cords. Those reeds vibrate, creating a vibrating column of air—the sound of the voice, shaped by the space that contains it: the throat, the mouth, the cavities of the skull. It's up to the singer to make a good home for the sound, to "place" it so every pitch resonates freely.

Singing is a physical art, and the most physical part of it is managing the flow of breath. I knew enough to take good deep breaths that expanded my abdomen, but I didn't understand how to use the abdominal muscles to push the breath, and the sound, out into the world. It was the cardinal thing I should have learned from Miss Pinnell.

At my first real lesson, she did what countless voice teachers have done before and since: she took my hand and placed it on her solar plexus and said, "Ha. Ha. Ha. Ha." Her figure was thick and matronly, but her abdomen was firm. I could feel a slight outward movement on each Ha. Or maybe it was an inward movement. This was a very important distinction: what, exactly, was the abdomen supposed to do? Her muscles were all working together, and mine hadn't a clue.

I sang some Ha Ha Has and some Hee Hee Hees. The Hees were focused and strong, but the Has were breathy. Then we worked on "Ridente La Calma" with its tangles of consonants.

Eager to show off my D'Oyly Carte diction, I articulated each word as clearly as I could, not understanding that in singing, vowels carry the sound, and consonants interrupt it. What I thought was good diction was snuffing out my voice.

It had been easy to learn the notes and words of this aria, but now I struggled with it. Standing next to the piano with Miss Pinnell at the keyboard, I had the humiliating realization that my singing was mediocre.

Over the previous year and a half of being coached by Miss Rigsbee, I'd been her shining star. My killer audition piece had been Mozart's "Alleluia," which is just that one word, alleluia, sung over and over, with coloratura runs and a high C at the end. I nailed that C—it was right in my wheelhouse. I nailed the runs, too, though I realize now that I wasn't supporting them properly. The piece worked for me because it lay in a high range where my voice was naturally bright. The songs I worked on with Miss Pinnell lay lower, where the problems were. In the octave between middle C and the C above it, my voice was patchy and unreliable.

This is not unusual. I can even tell you what causes it. (Bear with me.) The vocal cords produce different patterns of vibrations: one pattern for the lower range of notes, another for the middle range, and a third for the higher range. These ranges are called registers, and each register has a characteristic sound. I'm simplifying this, but the upshot is that as a singer goes from lower notes to higher ones, the shape of the vocal cords changes, and so does the quality of the sound.

The challenge is that there are audible breaks between registers. I think of them as gear shifts because they sound like an engine shifting gears. It's not pretty. It's yodeling—the sound of a voice switching back and forth between one register and another.

When I got to Miss Pinnell's studio, my registers weren't talking to each other. There were low notes that resonated in the chest, high notes that resonated in the head, and middle notes that were weak and breathy—the notes at the heart of the soprano range. Try as I might, I couldn't make those notes sound properly.

Miss Pinnell could hear this, of course, and she thought she knew how to fix it. She had me sing in Italian because Italian vowels are open, without diphthongs—the basis of beautiful singing. If she'd taught me to produce those vowel sounds correctly and support them with proper use of the breath, I would have seen my voice come together, gain focus, and start to grow. I know this because it happened in my thirties when I finally found the right teacher.

Miss Pinnell, however, never succeeded in showing me what the abdominal muscles are supposed to do, and those muscles are everything. They do the work of propelling the breath so the throat can stay open and relaxed. If you've ever watched a cat's belly as it meows, you've seen how naturally those muscles can produce sound. But cats live happily in their bodies, and I barely occupied mine. As I sang Miss Pinnell's unproductive exercises and mouthed those foreign texts, my voice seemed to become smaller and weaker. I began to feel something like despair.

21

WHITE KITTEN

A SINGER IS ENDOWED WITH a physical instrument: a larynx of a certain size, a throat and skull of a certain configuration, and a pair of lungs with a certain capacity. These are gifts of God or heredity or dumb luck, depending on your point of view, but they are gifts. For some kinds of singing, the physical instrument doesn't matter much. You can sing into a microphone and do just fine. But I aspired to sing with my naked natural voice, and I needed to be able to fill a theater with it.

I told myself I didn't want to be an opera singer because G&S isn't opera, it's *light* opera, and I'd been told I had a light voice. Which is nonsense. What I really wanted was to sing like Ann Drummond-Grant, and her voice was operatic—rich, powerful, beautifully trained. She'd had to train it twice, first as a soprano and later, when her voice deepened, as a contralto. Even in Gilbert's patter songs with their fusillades of rapid-fire words, her shining sound came through, thrilling at the top, commanding at the bottom, clean and penetrating in the middle, with no audible gear shifts in between. She had a fine natural instrument, but it was furious discipline that made her a singer.

I had a commonplace sort of voice, a lyric soprano, light and true. No one told me it would ever be a big voice, but everyone said I was musical—meaning that when I sang a song, I made music of it, shaped the phrases, kept the listener listening. My high notes rang out: *Yay! Wow! I'm a singer!* But the lower notes disappeared. I hated that, was mortified by it. I had a profound conviction that there was a voice in there somewhere, and that training would bring it out. I believed this because Miss Rigs-bee believed it, and because Ann Drummond-Grant was such a living presence in my life. Surely, *she* wanted it for me. I shaped words with her voice in my ear, using the Scottish inflections that were dear to my heart but seldom appropriate to the music. A word like *tears* became *teeeearrs*, long and dramatic with the *r* slightly rolled.

It wasn't many months before Miss Pinnell leveled with me. My voice, she told me with flat Midwestern candor, was not developing as she'd expected. "When you haven't got it, it's a bitter pill to swallow," she said. "But it's better and kinder that I tell you now, before you go any further down this road." She smiled a grim sympathetic smile and told me to go home and "think about it."

Think about *what?* Miss Rigsbee had always said I was her best; she treated me like a musician in training. And the dead singer for whom I was doing all this, whose name I wrote in my notebooks like a prayer, was still calling to me. But my faith in my own talent was fragile. Miss Pinnell was the authority, a professor of singing at Syracuse University, and if she told me I didn't "have it," I was supposed to believe her. That left me with no purpose, no future, no life.

I couldn't believe that a dream as imperative as mine could end so abruptly and humiliatingly. And I couldn't bear to tell anyone—certainly not my parents, who I assumed would take Miss Pinnell's word for it. I needed strength. I went to the strongest woman I knew, Mrs. Metosh. At the end of my next Latin class, I asked if I could talk to her and collapsed like a child, pouring out my grief to this woman with the least musi-cal, most stentorian voice I knew.

She sat and listened quietly, large and formidable in her invariable sleeveless dress and cloud of Estée Lauder scent. When I finished, she did not offer bromides. "My daughter, Vickie, breeds lilac point Siamese cats," she said. "When those kitties are born, they're completely white. Their points—the mask, the ears, the paws—only get dark with time. And the breeder just can't know whether a given kitty is going to develop the markings of a champion. The breeder has a lot riding on this. But she just has to wait and see how they develop.

"You're like one of those white kittens. There's no telling how you're going to turn out at this point. But you're still growing. All you can do is work and wait and have faith that it will all turn out well."

She smiled. "Yep, you're still a white kitten."

It was such a relief to be a white kitten. To know that nothing was settled, and that Mrs. Metosh had faith in me, not necessarily as a singer, but as a person. That there was still time and room to grow.

Deeply encouraged, I marched right back to the one person who consistently demonstrated a lack of faith in me: Miss Pinnell. I told her I wanted to continue—to work hard and see how the voice developed. If she wished I had decided otherwise, she gave no sign of it.

It soon came out that, in my previous lessons, I hadn't sung low notes with the deeper, larger voice that resonated in my chest. I didn't use that voice—the chest register—because I thought it was the sound of a rock singer or a Broadway belter, not a classical soprano. But trying to sing without the chest register is like trying to stand without legs; it's key for developing and unifying all the registers of the voice. When I inadvertently let out some hefty low notes one day, Miss Pinnell said, "Where has *that* voice been?"

"I didn't know I was supposed to use it," I said, like the white kitten I was.

"Of *course* you're supposed to use it," she said, genuinely annoyed.

So the chest register came into the mix, and my voice began to sound better. But between that robust low register and the weaker middle one, there was still a terrible shifting of gears, which Miss Pinnell couldn't seem to train me out of. Nevertheless, we both acted like I was finally on the royal road to good singing.

22

THE BOY
FROM HAMBURG

As always, I was split in two. There was the person I presented to the world: a young singer, snarky and outspoken, sure of her talent, quickness of mind, and purity of purpose. And there was the hot mess under the mask, a cripplingly shy girl-woman in a sweaty body that jiggled where it shouldn't and was racked, seemingly every ten minutes, by menstrual cramps. Deeper than the waves of pain were the waves of need, thus far unanswered, to be seen and known and loved. I couldn't imagine being loved in this body unless I could somehow talk or sing my way into it.

I had reason to believe my body was unlovable. I'd never been held or cuddled. My brothers and I had been cared for, provided for, and cleaned up after, but soft words and physical affection had we none. Mother, a constant peevish presence in the house, was, in a deeper sense, absent. She was attractive enough, funny enough, intelligent enough that we all thought we could find a way of presenting ourselves that would please her. But the things that mattered to us didn't interest her. So we were on our own. I was on my own.

I was embarrassed to sing when Mother was in the house. I wasn't good enough. I want to add that she never gave me a word of encouragement. Actually, she might have. But if she did, I didn't take it in; I was too frantic about my lack of progress. The scales and vocalises assigned by Miss Pinnell did not improve with repetition. The songs I worked on had the same stubborn problems in the same places. I needed to practice more! But I'd begun to hate practicing.

Worse, I'd fallen so hard for music that I couldn't imagine devoting my life to anything else. And this time it wasn't because of Ann Drummond-Grant, whom I still loved dearly. I'd fallen for Brahms.

Brahms was the boyfriend I never had. Not the man—short, caustic, aggressively bearded, cigar-smoking, deceased—but the music. I responded to the passion and sheer beauty of it. Brahms was a Romantic composer, and I was a romantic sort of girl, in the literal sense of feeling jammed full of emotion I had no outlet for. I wrote down a quote from the twenty-six-year-old composer: "I am in love with music, I love music, I think of nothing but, and of other things only when they make music more beautiful for me. . . . If it continues like this, I may evaporate into a chord and float off into the air."

That was exactly how I felt. But I also wrote down another quote from the young Brahms: "Passions are not natural to mankind; they are always exceptions or excrescences. The ideal, genuine man is calm in joy and calm in pain and sorrow. Passions must quickly pass, or else they must be driven out." I didn't quite buy this; it sounded like he was trying to talk himself down. But it did reveal something about the elegant structures he built to contain all that feeling.

I didn't realize, as I listened to my brother Julian's records—he was in Stuttgart on a post-graduate fellowship in chemistry—that I was getting an education in classical form. Brahms's music is beautiful not just because the melodies, harmonies, and rhythms are pleasing, but because it's masterfully

THAT VOICE

crafted. The tighter and more disciplined the structure, the greater the effect of freedom and spontaneity. I wasn't aware of this at the time, but those structures burned themselves into my brain as templates for a life of listening.

I could see that not everyone responded to Brahms as I did. It seemed to me that everyone who enters into the love of music does so through a particular door. It took me years to appreciate Mozart, and slogging through Wagner hasn't rewarded me yet. But Brahms grabbed me from the start.

He carried me through the last two interminable years at Nottingham High—through the general anarchy, the cynicism and rage of the student body, the constant police presence, and my own chronic alienation and humiliation. Brahms was always in my head: the chamber music, the solo piano music, the symphonies. I hid out in the B-flat Piano Concerto for days at a time. I made Miss Pinnell give me Brahms to sing and begged Mrs. Tannenbaum for anything of his to play, though he was beyond my technique. She assigned me one of the short late pieces, and I practiced it with blissful obsessiveness until I mastered it, or thought I did.

In my senior year, to my astonishment, I felt attracted to a boy my own age. He was quiet and clean-cut and acted strange around me, as though he were trying to decide whether he liked me enough to say so. I said nothing. But there were days when I'd lie on my bed listening to Brahms and fantasizing that he and I might one day listen thus together, fingers entwined. That was as far as the fantasy went. Whatever this boy felt or didn't feel, he already had a girlfriend, someone petite and self-confident. The minute I realized this, I shut down my attraction. It never occurred to me to flirt with him. I didn't know how.

There was another boy that year who clearly was attracted to me. He called me nightly to talk about things he thought would interest me while I sat silent on the other end. "Let's see . . . what else?" he'd say, moving from one topic to the next. (He must have made lists.) I liked Ray. He had kind, pale-green eyes and, under the acne, a shy Jewish face: hooked nose, prominent jaw, slightly snaggled teeth. A pleasing face. And he was smart—a reader, a music lover. He had an older brother in the Bronx, and he carried with him that New York worldliness that seemed to me what real life must be about. His mother kept a kosher home, she told me, at her sons' behest; she herself had not been raised to be observant. The observance was the rub. Ray wore a kippah, kept the Sabbath, and seemed to find real joy in his Jewishness. I might have tried to find it too, if I could have induced myself to feel the least bit attracted to him physically. But he was tall and slender, almost frail, the sort who looked like he could be knocked over. It unnerved me to be wanted by him.

He never stood a chance. I was addicted to the idea of love-as-thunderclap, and the thunder had already struck in April of my junior year. It possessed my soul but bypassed my body almost entirely. Which was just the way I wanted it.

23

THUNDERCLAP

THE OCCASION WAS A RECITAL at Crouse College by the newest member of the SU piano faculty, Frederick Marvin. I don't remember why I went; Miss Pinnell might have suggested it. He was said to be several cuts above the local talent, a concert pianist with an active career in Europe. There was a shimmer to the way people spoke about him. When he crossed the stage of Crouse Auditorium, I saw a shortish, middle-aged man with longish brown hair, formally attired. The minute he started playing, I was done.

Why, exactly? I didn't ask. When it comes to thunderclaps, "Why?" is not the first question. I was aware that his playing had a rightness to it. The technique was strong, without stumbles. He made beautiful sounds, a whole palette of them. More importantly, he understood what the composer was saying—structurally and emotionally—and could convey it to the listener. He was, in other words, the real thing. I had heard good pianists before, but I'd never been in the same room with one who spoke to me like *that*.

I don't remember the whole program, but I know he began with Padre Antonio Soler, an eighteenth-century Spanish composer I'd never heard of. Fred had achieved a degree of fame, including a Spanish knighthood, for bringing Soler's music to light, and I found it charming. Better than charming. Soler studied with Domenico Scarlatti, and his keyboard sonatas, more than two hundred in number, are playful, surprising, and harmonically daring. Fred played them with enormous style.

He might also have played Chopin and possibly Beethoven. To this day, some of Fred's performances of those composers' works are in my head, indelible. When he was good, he was damn good. When he was off, he could be awful, but I had no inkling of that yet. Fred was my perfect man—charismatic, older, and unattainable—my trifecta. His performance set in motion an odd sequence of events with huge consequences.

I wasn't the only person in town who was taken with Fred. He was lionized by most (but not all) of the local music community—especially the more prominent female piano teachers, who vied with each other to befriend him and send him their best students. They brought him cheesecake and strawberries and bulbs for his garden; they threw dinner parties for him and took him antique shopping. He, in turn, held musical soirees at the modest house he was gradually turning into a little showplace.

My piano teacher didn't run in such circles. She taught little kids. But I had a classmate at Nottingham who studied with one of those prominent teachers. She'd been completely off my radar, but I somehow heard that she was doing yard work for Fred, and I became determined, desperate, to work there with her. Never mind that I'd never done a lick of yard work. This girl, whoever she was, had to become my friend.

Her name was Lisa, and she was ostentatiously friendly, a friendliness that masked deep shyness. When I asked her about Fred, she called him Doctor Marvin (he didn't have a doctorate) and, in a high, clear voice, told me several things in rapid succession: He was friends with her piano teacher, Mrs. Sack. He had obtained a Hamburg Steinway for Mrs. Sack, and Hamburg Steinways were the best pianos in the world, better than

American Steinways, and through Mrs. Sack, he had obtained one for her, too, a ten-thousand-dollar instrument at a significant discount, and she was so grateful she was mowing his lawn with a little hand mower that was better than a power mower because his lawn was on a hill, and in back there was a terraced garden, and she was weeding that by hand.

I asked if I could help. Lisa was clearly every bit as gone on Fred as I was and could, by rights, have been possessive about working for him, but she said yes, gulping a little. I could see she was willing herself to be generous. She had grown up in a tough part of town, way over on North Salina Street, and been picked on mercilessly as a tiny, scrawny kid. Somewhere along the line, she'd vowed to show others the kindness that had not been shown to her. When she disagreed with you, she'd always listen respectfully before sharing her point of view, chapter and verse, in that high, clear voice that I heard quite a lot of in the ensuing years.

I believed myself more sophisticated than Lisa, but we were like any other teenage girls with a crush on the same boy, or in this case, fifty-year-old man. We talked endlessly about him, the music he played, and how beautifully he played it. Lisa's crush was more overt than mine. Her whole family talked and teased about Fred—they talked easily with each other, not something I was used to. I didn't talk about Fred at my house, any more than I talked about Ann Drummond-Grant. Lisa had an LP of Fred playing Soler which we listened to over and over, sprawled at either end of the long sectional couch in her living room. It really was very good playing, sprightly and precise and somehow masculine. What sent me into paroxysms of jealousy was that Mrs. Sack had assigned Lisa one of these very sonatas, and I had to listen to her practice it. As though she'd gotten to take communion, and I hadn't.

Lisa's parents weren't especially well off—it may be more accurate to say that, with four children to educate, they spent their money carefully. The new Hamburg Steinway was the most magnificent thing in the house, possibly the most magnificent thing in the neighborhood. Over six feet long with a shining black lacquer finish, it stood in the dining room where the table would have been, covered by a blanket. It made the most beautiful sounds I'd ever heard from a piano: soft, round, harp-like, yet strong and clear.

The small upright piano Lisa had grown up with, painted dark green and red in a sort of Navajo pattern, stood at the end of the room, ready for business, scores open on the music stand. Lisa practiced on that, moving to the Steinway by degrees, as one might move from a beat-up Chevy to a new Mercedes. She'd roll back the blanket and open the music stand, usually leaving the lid closed, rarely propping it halfway open with the short stick. She'd fiddle with the height of the new quilted bench, the kind real pianists used. She'd take a large handkerchief and stow it on the tuning pins behind the music stand so she could periodically wipe the keys with it—she was self-conscious about her sweaty hands. She'd play her big piece, the Chopin Scherzo in C-sharp minor. And then she'd play it again. And again. I heard her play that eight-minute piece so many times that the sound of its first bars still makes me grit my teeth, though she played it well.

It is a hugely difficult piece, full of demonic octaves, treacherous left-hand leaps, and cascading arpeggios. The fact that she could play it at all marked her as a serious student worthy of a good instrument. I'd never met anyone who practiced harder than Lisa. I didn't know that any serious pianist practices at least that hard.

Lisa's previous big piece had been Mendelssohn's Andante and Rondo Capriccioso, and she was convinced in her generous way that I would be able to play it too, if I studied it with Mrs. Sack and practiced it slowly. She lent me the music. The first page, the Andante, I could play almost at sight. The rest was quicksilver fast and way beyond my capabilities. But I liked the idea of studying with Mrs. Sack, who was not just one of the best teachers in town but a close friend of Fred Marvin. Lisa was sure she'd be willing to take me on, even at my level.

I made an appointment to play for her.

24

MRS. SACK AND
THE CHURCH OF FRED

HAD I BEEN MORE PLUGGED in to the Syracuse music establishment, I'd have heard of Lucille Sack, a Juilliard-trained pianist who was also the city's only serious harpsichordist. She lived near the university in a square old bluish-gray house that looked somewhat forbidding. The entrance was on the driveway side. I rang the bell. She opened the door and informed me, as she led me through a tiny vestibule into a proper entrance hall, that "in this house, nobody rings the doorbell. Just walk right in." This seemed sensible, considering that students came and went all afternoon long. But in fact, it was a broader policy: only tradesmen and strangers ever rang that bell. Everyone else breezed in, accompanied by the whoosh of the door and their extended "Hello!"

Mrs. Sack was a short woman of fifty-one, ample of bosom and slender of waist, with cropped black hair and a clear alto voice. Brusque and welcoming, she drew me into her abundant, orderly life without ceremony. Her tiny living room held two grand pianos. Tucked into a corner of the dining room was a small, sleek harpsichord with two stacked manuals, the white keys black and vice versa. A surprising amount of light flowed into what I'd thought would be a dark house.

I sat at her German Steinway, every bit as glorious as Lisa's, and played the Brahms Intermezzo I was so proud of. Its right-hand part consists of chords with a melody at the bottom; I hit those notes with my thumb. She said, "Well, dear, that's not bad, but it's actually meant to be played *this* way"—and she showed me how the melody was supposed to be legato, with the notes connected—which meant playing it with the thumb and forefinger while the other fingers played a softer accompaniment. Suddenly the piece was beyond my technique. "There's no point in your relearning this," she said. "We'll start with something new."

It seemed clear that Mrs. Tannenbaum hadn't taught the piece properly. But it's more likely she knew my limitations and wanted to let me play it as best I could. I'd started piano lessons at fourteen. There were years of technique I hadn't acquired, years that couldn't be made up for. But there could still be love and pleasure and real improvement: a world of music in my hands. With singing, there was the constant fear I would never measure up.

Mrs. Tannenbaum was gracious when I told her I wanted to study with Mrs. Sack. "I've probably taken you about as far as I can," she said. I wonder if this was true.

Mrs. Sack got right down to business. She had me order Bach's Two-Part Inventions in the Peters Urtext Edition. From my battered old Kalmus edition of Brahms, she assigned a slower, easier piece than the one I'd mangled. She played it through for me and then said what struck me as magic words: "Here's how I want you to practice this." No one had said that to me before, or shown me how to break down technical challenges into short, manageable drills. She gave me mimeographed sheets of fingerings for major and minor scales in all keys, written out in her large, clear script, and showed me how they made physiological sense.

Did I want to play scales? Of course I did. It was a way for my hands to learn their way around the keyboard, for my fingers to start catching up with my music-besotted brain. It was exactly the sort of instruction I wasn't getting from Miss Pinnell, who saw my vocal deficiencies but couldn't guide me out of them. It's arguably harder to teach vocal technique than piano technique. But not if you know what you're doing.

That summer of 1970, I practiced four hours a day for Mrs. Sack, starting with an hour of scales. Veins started popping up on the backs of my hands—piano hands, she called them. I was proud of those veins. (Now, they merely look grandmotherly.) I also practiced singing—Miss Pinnell was back home in rural Illinois for the summer—but halfheartedly. My voice tired quickly and never seemed to grow stronger or surer because I was doing the same wrong things over and over. At the piano, my work paid off. When I strained my right wrist wielding a trowel in Fred Marvin's garden, Mrs. Sack gave me exercises for the left hand.

I had no idea how to use that trowel. But I had to do *something* while Lisa pushed her ancient mower back and forth across Fred's front lawn. I worked on the terraces of neglected flower beds in back, turning the soil and removing anything that struck me as weedlike. God knows what I took out of those beds that might have belonged there. Fred himself was off concertizing and not due back till late July, so Lisa and I had free rein to prettify the place. She befriended the neighbors, whom she genuinely liked—Lisa always found reasons to like people—and of course told Mrs. Sack about her mission of gratitude. Mrs. Sack raised an eyebrow but knew enough to let Lisa be Lisa. She was quite fond of Fred herself, and we weren't doing any harm, though when we planted tulip bulbs, we put them in upside down.

I don't believe I'd even shaken hands with Fred at that point. It was enough to be working in the holy yard of the holy house, a tiny, shingled Cape Cod built in the midforties. Fred had knocked out the back wall and raised the roof to create a concert space with a cathedral ceiling. He'd commissioned abstract stained-glass windows for what used to be the top floor, and their jewel-toned light fell on the two nested grand pianos (shiny black, like Lisa's) and the oriental rugs. I could only view this space by looking in from the outside but was deeply impressed. It was the Church of Fred, and it became the center of my universe for the entire year I was supposed to be applying to colleges and getting ready to face the world.

Like the Church of Ann Drummond-Grant, the Church of Fred was built around an ideal of perfection, fealty to which kept me pure and lit a pilgrim's path through life. This notion of becoming a singer—truth to tell, I was no longer sure about it. I needed to be good, really good. Not because I craved an adoring audience—I didn't—but because I'd experienced what singing could do for the soul, and I believed in the soul. I kept waiting for something to happen. But my voice, scrabbling through thickets of German and French in "sublime" art songs, was a slender thing, a place marker.

So what, exactly, was I doing? Keeping my promise to Ann Drummond-Grant. In sneaking over to the Church of Fred, I felt like I was cheating on her. But adoration was my natural state, and Fred wasn't a bad object for it. When he returned home to find that two smitten teenage girls had tended his yard and generally improved it, he expressed a careful gratitude, though he couldn't help pointing out that we'd trimmed a couple of young spruce trees too aggressively. ("You cut the lead branch, dear," he told Lisa, who withered visibly.) Mrs. Sack must have let him know what we were doing, so he was fully prepared to be lionized. Also, we worked for free.

To me, Fred seemed immeasurably cultured and worldly. Every time I saw him, I felt that same thunderclap. I had not, at seventeen, read Dante, but I filled my notebooks with the same tropes of courtly love Dante used to write about Beatrice: the transcendent beauty of the beloved's eyes and smile. Fred's eyes, brown with green in them, were sad and kind and a bit tired, with small pouches underneath. And his smile seemed the visual equivalent of the opening of Schumann's Fantasie in C for piano: a burst of color, a door opening on a bright realm of feeling. Though I noted that his teeth were slightly yellow.

Unlike Ann Drummond-Grant, Fred still had a body, and that body was not unattractive. He was a bit taller than me and compactly built, with the quiet strength that comes from decades of serious piano practice. I didn't have a strong physical response to him but—as usual with me—felt something emotional and spiritual. I wanted to be overmastered by such feelings.

There was a night around this time when, unable to sleep, I battled with myself about believing in God and—another thunderclap—fell into deep, joyful weeping, silently repeating, "The Lord is my shepherd" over and over. It was a conversion experience that didn't linger long in the light of day, but it was of a piece with my adoration of Fred. He had become the godlike presence who heard my thoughts and blessed them—or didn't—the exalted being whose love I needed to win by being brighter and better and purer. I lived with some version of this presence for decades, finding successive people to embody it. I always thought it was love, and it always was, but the deeper truth was that I didn't feel complete in myself. How old was I when I finally knew the bliss of being alone and happy in my own head? Over forty. As old as Katisha.

25

VENT VERT

I CAN ADMIRE FRED NOW for finding the right way to address us, the right distance to keep, the right sort of noblesse oblige. And I can say that for the next forty-seven years—he lived a long time—he was never less than kind and affectionate. But at the beginning, this was a problem. I was gone on him, and he was nice to me.

I tended his yard till the snow fell and baked him brownies thereafter. I noted that he welcomed a stream of visitors—singers, students, friends—but went to concerts alone. I watched for him at the symphony and at Crouse College (where both he and Miss Pinnell taught), doing my best to sparkle and scintillate, still convinced that being ostentatiously clever was the key to being loved. When I encountered him, he called me "sweetheart" or "dear" (pronounced *deah*) and entered willingly into silly banter, a few moments of which could sustain me for a week.

Lisa, too, suffered over Fred, and it was tougher for her because she planned to study with him at SU and was preparing for her audition. Her whole future seemed to depend on succeeding. I had no doubt he would accept her as a student, but she lacked the confidence to believe it herself. She was easily shot down. But I sensed her toughness and strength of purpose. Even in despair, Lisa always persevered.

I had less at stake. No one expected my voice to be mature. Singers don't come into their own till their thirties, or so I'd been told. I had a bedrock belief that my voice would grow and was determined to go to music school and major in vocal performance. Preferably not at Syracuse University. But I could attend Syracuse and keep studying with Miss Pinnell if I didn't get into the conservatory of my choice, whatever that was. I didn't want to think about it, though it was very much time to do so.

I ruled out the top-tier conservatories. I was sure Juilliard wouldn't take me and was probably right. I styled myself as a singer of art songs and oratorio, though I lacked the experience to specialize and strongly suspected there was no way to make a living at either. I just needed to call myself *something*.

I resisted applying to colleges with all my might. My parents nagged me but offered no direction, and I might not have taken it if they had. The school guidance counselors were useless. But the older sister of someone in my Latin class was attending Oberlin College and liking it, and Oberlin had a fine conservatory. I fixed on the idea of going there. Surely an artsy school like that, way out in Ohio (i.e., the middle of nowhere) would welcome an art song singer. As usual, I had no idea how competitive the real world was. Oberlin was the only place I applied other than Syracuse, my safety school.

Once I got the applications out of the way, I returned to what I liked best. Listening to classical music. Writing in my notebook. Practicing the piano for Mrs. Sack, who assigned pieces that were increasingly challenging but always within reach: Bach, Brahms, Chopin, Beethoven, Soler. She seemed to enjoy teaching me as much as I enjoyed studying with her. I remember her vigorously stretching my fingers as she talked to me about a piece, a gesture both efficient and affectionate. She literally took me in hand. She wore a sublime fragrance called *Vent Vert*, a clear green floral unlike anything I'd ever smelled.

I'd buy a bottle now if I could, but the version she wore, created in 1947, is long gone. In fact, she outlived it.

Lucille (as I soon began calling her) drove a heavy black station wagon large enough to hold her harpsichord and its tuning paraphernalia. It wasn't long before that wagon was pulling up in front of my house to carry me on one adventure or another. Some were musical—rehearsals, coaching sessions with a local soprano—but there were also shopping expeditions for antiques she could refinish or refurbish, quests for plants for her wild-looking garden or for foods I'd never heard of. She showed me how to cook bok choy, which did not appear on the table of anyone else I knew.

If Mother was jealous of the time I spent with Lucille, and I came to realize much later that she was, she never said so. Nor did she comment when I bought a bottle of *Vent Vert* and gave it pride of place on my dresser. But Lucille appreciated things in me that Mother seemed not to: that I was musical, articulate, passionate. Passion was my signal quality, the big thing I knew about myself. It was what I recognized in Ann Drummond-Grant and how I knew her as kin. The same went for Brahms and, I suppose, for Fred. With very little provocation, passion slopped over into melodrama. My notebooks from that time are hard to read; they go on and on about how alive I am. It begins to sound desperate.

Lucille understood the passion and put up with the melodrama, to a point. Her approach to all problems, musical and otherwise, was deeply practical. She could always get me to stop emoting and start thinking. Thinking was a relief. I could see my way out of a jam if I could manage to get my head on straight. Mrs. Metosh had told me the same thing.

Lucille did her sensible best to talk me out of my crush on Fred. I knew she was right—that there was no future in it, that it was childish and beside the point. I had never even imagined being kissed by this man who, as far as I could tell, was married to his piano. Neither of us mentioned Ernst, Fred's manager, who was then in Vienna but stayed with Fred when he was in town. I'd met Ernst. Same height and build as Fred; same dazzling smile (though Ernst was blonde and wore glasses with pink-tinted lenses). He seemed nice, but his English was poor and his Viennese accent impenetrable. I hadn't managed a real conversation with him.

Fred went off to Europe for months at a time, which put me in my preferred state of long-distance obsession. I had things to do. There was the Oberlin audition to prepare for. Before that, I auditioned for the voice faculty at Syracuse University, Miss Pinnell included. She told me I was a lot better than the others they'd been hearing. (She actually seemed to like me now.) Oh, and that little rasp in my voice? She was sure it would go away with work and maturity.

I wasn't so sure. When I practiced singing, it seemed a mockery, I didn't feel like a real musician. Thirty sit-ups a night, I'd heard, would improve my muscle tone, but I felt unmotivated to do them. Was my voice even worth training? It had to be.

Miss Pinnell had a reputation as a good teacher. Her own soprano voice seemed impressive to me, large if somewhat colorless. Lucille said, "I gather she had a beautiful voice that lost its bloom early." I couldn't get past that remark. It was one of the memorably bitchy things Lucille couldn't stop herself from saying.

Admission to Oberlin Conservatory depended entirely on my audition; it didn't matter that my grades were good and my SAT scores high. I traveled there alone, by plane and taxi. The audition was in the new music building, Bibbins Hall, a fantastical structure clad in a Gothic-inspired lacework of steel and quartz. The architect, clearly entranced with it, used a similar lacy facade for his next project, the World Trade Center, so it's jarring to see the place now. At the time, I was dazzled by its many practice rooms stocked with brand new Steinways. The practice rooms at SU were few, the pianos beaten beyond repair.

I was dead ignorant about my target school. I stayed on campus just one night, sleeping on the floor of my classmate's sister's dorm room. When I remarked on the cold, she told me winters there were about as bad as winters in Syracuse. I hadn't researched the conservatory's voice or piano faculty; no one had recommended a particular teacher. At my audition, I sang (pretty damn well, I thought) a song by Fauré, for which a decent accompanist was provided. There was a sight-singing test. And then I made the long trip home, having spoken at length to nobody except Ann Drummond-Grant, in my own head. The audition was an offering to her. I believed I was following the path she'd set for me. Without her, there was no path at all.

26

EDINBURGH, 1904

ABOUT THE LADY HERSELF, I knew almost nothing. For decades, I had only the sound of her voice, and that had to be enough. My beloved G&S books contained scant trace of her except for the small black-and-white photos that dissolved into random dots under a magnifying glass. But by my forty-fifth birthday, there was an internet. There was Google, where Gilbert and Sullivan geeks could seek each other out, and, soon after, Wikipedia, where not-always-reliable information began accruing. Most internet sources said that Ann Drummond-Grant was born in Edinburgh (correct) in 1905 (incorrect).

Even in middle age, I could barely bring myself to write her name, let alone speak it. But there were people I needed to ask about her. Tony Joseph, who wrote a definitive history of the D'Oyly Carte Company. Chris Webster, who brilliantly remastered her recordings and released them on CD. Both were generous about sharing information and putting me in touch with people who'd known her. Public records began to be accessible online. She seemed to be casting a trail of small, luminous clues.

It was through Chris Webster that I first heard her low, musical speaking voice, in a radio interview she did in San Francisco in 1955. Asked by the fawning interviewer about what led her to join the D'Oyly Carte, she said, "I had quite a bit of vocal training, and did quite a lot of oratorio work, and broadcasting . . . and then I had a *desire* to take up the stage. . . ."

That last bit is an understatement. Digging through public records to glean what I could about her, I learned that she couldn't have escaped the life she was born into if she hadn't wanted that stage career with all her might. And that she had to wait what seemed an eternity to make it happen.

The Edinburgh of her childhood was a straitlaced and proper place bound by a church whose Calvinist austerity was seen as a mark of moral superiority. To a sensitive spirit, it was also a magical place. I'm not imagining this. I've walked the streets where she lived as a child and been carried by the rhythm of those hills falling to the sea. Glacial hills, like the hills of Syracuse, but even hillier. Smack in the middle of town sits the core of an extinct volcano, Arthur's Seat, a wild open space where you can climb high enough to see for miles. On the opposite hill, the other end of the original lava flow, sits Edinburgh Castle, once home to medieval kings and besieged and bombarded ever after. Winter nights are so long and dark it becomes necessary to rely on your own inner light. Summer nights, endlessly bright, give you the fuel to do it.

At least one of Ann Drummond-Grant's childhood homes had a view of Arthur's Seat. All of them were in high places, on blocks of small, attached houses or tenements in the tidy terraces of the New Town. Because of how they're situated, these terraces manage to be both depressing and exhilarating.

She didn't come from money. Far from it. Her father, Alexander Grant, an upholsterer's son, was a commercial traveler. These were manufacturers' representatives who peddled products to shopkeepers, covering large territories and making many sales calls per week. Usually they were paid a salary and expenses, with commissions kicking in above a certain sales level. Some, depending on the goods they sold, earned a decent enough living to lift their families out of the working class. But many aspired to middle-class status without achieving it.

Alexander Grant worked in the drapery trade, which, being fashion-oriented, tended to be seasonal. This tells me two things: The family income was not steady. And the man of the house was absent for long stretches.

The lady of the house, Jean Grant, was a livestock farmer's daughter, doubtless a good Church of Scotland girl. She produced two daughters: Agnes, born in March 1901, and our Ann, born in November 1904. Ann's given name was Annie Drummond Grant, but she seems never to have been called Annie. She was always "Drummie." When I first learned this, I couldn't square the name with her regal bearing, her magnificent sadness, her enormous stage presence. Offstage, though, "Drummie" seems to have suited her, plain and simple, the nickname of a woman without pretensions.

The Grants were a working-class family. The census of 1901 lists Alexander, Jean, and baby Agnes, plus a medical nurse. Ten years later, in a slightly larger flat, there were the two parents, their two daughters, and Jean's younger sister Agnes, presumably there to help. There may have been other part-time help—a maid, a cook. In those days, you hired what help you could afford and did the rest yourself. This is according to Naomi Sim (wife of the actor Alastair Sim), who grew up in Edinburgh around that time. She says in her lyrical memoir that to call yourself middle-class, you had to have at least two live-in servants and rooms to put them in. The Grants had neither.

There were limits to the amount of housework Drummie's mother could do. Jean Grant's heart had been damaged when she was two years old, most likely by rheumatic fever following an attack of strep. As a result, she had chronic bronchitis all her life, along with an increased susceptibility to infection. She might have possessed a fine singing voice like her daughter's, but she wouldn't have been able to draw proper breath to support it. I like to think that Drummie's singing was a particular delight to her.

Here's what would have happened: Drummie would have gone to church, of course, and sung in a Sunday school choir where her voice stood out, pure and clear. The choir director would have said, "This is a talent that must be nurtured." And Drummie would have discovered that she loved to sing, loved the effect her voice had on people. It must have been magical from the very beginning, standing at the center of that sound.

Sometime in October 1918, during the second wave of the great pandemic, Jean Grant came down with the Spanish Flu. She died six weeks later—fourteen days after the Armistice—after developing endocarditis, an infection of the heart. She was forty-two. Three months later to the day, Jean's mother, Drummie's grandmother, also died of the flu.

Drummie had just turned fourteen. Her sister Agnes was seventeen. They were, in effect, orphaned, left to run the household while their father traveled and to care for him while he was home. Left to do the cooking and cleaning and mending their mother had done, in the absence of the love she'd given them. When they got old enough to work, they went to work. They had to. Drummie must have found it gratifying when she began to get paid to sing, but she can't have made much money at it.

When her mother died, Drummie was trapped. She might not have felt that way at first, in the overwhelmingness of the event. Having a mother in poor health would have accustomed her to helping with the housework and being a good, quiet daughter. She'd have done her share of caregiving: Drummie was an inveterate nurturer all her life. But at fourteen, not long after puberty—which arrived much later in those days than it does now—large things were happening inside her. She was growing a woman's voice in a woman's body. She was beginning to know she wanted a singing career, and that it was not a dream but an imperative. Her mother's death meant that her desire to perform had to take a back seat to the needs of her family. And it meant something else: she couldn't let herself feel anger at her mother for leaving her. None of the usual adolescent upheaval could happen. You can't rebel against a sainted dead woman. You have to become a bit of a saint yourself.

There's no written record of this. But I see it in that fine sadness of hers and hear it in the passion and sympathy she brought to Gilbert's rejected women. There was a time in her life when she felt abandoned and brokenhearted; there was a sorrow that never left her. I recognized this at fifteen, when the devastating news of her death left me orphaned in a different way. I never felt for my mother what I felt for Ann Drummond-Grant.

Her father lived eleven more years, succumbing to laryngeal cancer at age sixty-two. (So there was tobacco smoke in that home.) The sisters remained in their tenement flat for another four years, until 1933, when Agnes got married and Drummie joined the D'Oyly Carte. They would have stayed together for two pressing reasons: they were devoted to each other, and their combined incomes supported the household. The flat was roomy for the two of them, now that it no longer housed a father who smoked and a mother who coughed: two bedrooms, parlor, kitchen and bath, with a little balcony in back to hang the washing.

Agnes was thirty-two and working as a secretary when she married. Drummie, at twenty-eight, had achieved a measure of local fame as a singer, having pursued every possible opportunity in her hometown. Here's how she's described in a D'Oyly Carte program from 1936:

> Ann Drummond-Grant, soprano, comes from Edinburgh where she studied singing under Miss Lind Horsburgh, a well-known Scottish contralto. For five years she was leading soprano in the South Leith Parish Church. Miss Drummond-Grant has played leading roles in *The Waltz Dream*, *The Marriage Market*, and also in the opera *Carmen*. She has done a considerable amount of radio singing and concert work. Three years ago, she joined the D'Oyly Carte Opera Company as a chorister. Her lovely voice soon attracted attention and gained for her early promotion.

I can find no trace of Miss Lind Horsburgh on the internet, but she was clearly an excellent teacher. *The Waltz Dream* and *The Marriage Market* were entertainments of the light Viennese sort. As for *Carmen*, Drummie might have had the vocal equipment for the title role, but I'm betting she was cast as the good-girl soprano Micaëla. She seems to have been a good girl indeed, focused and deeply serious about her vocation.

She was a strikingly attractive young woman: tall, lean, and shapely, with lively blue eyes and a warm smile. Her posture, then and always, was superb—Miss Horsburgh would have insisted on it. There's no knowing whether she had any serious romantic entanglements in her twenties. Agnes seems not to have; it took her four years to marry after their father died. This strikes me as strange. Girls in their twenties can be counted on to fall in love at least once. And I'm reliably informed that parish church choirs are hotbeds of romance.

27

THE LOWLAND SEA, 1971

SHORTLY AFTER MY OBERLIN AUDITION, I had my first and last leading role in an opera, a piece Miss Rigsbee had long wanted to stage called *The Lowland Sea*. Its composer, Alec Wilder, wrote popular songs, jazz-inflected chamber music, and a lot of what has to be called whatnot. *The Lowland Sea* was whatnot. Just fifty-five minutes long and designed for college students, it was a "folk drama" with songs that sounded almost like real folk music.

Real folk music is memorable. Some of Wilder's tunes have stuck in my head from sheer repetition, but they are completely ersatz, and so is the plot: Dorie Davis loves a sailor named Johnny Dee. He sails away; his ship goes down; she marries a widower with children; and Johnny, who was not drowned but put ashore with malaria, returns. They still love each other. He sails away. Curtain. The sailors sing faux chanteys and dance an approximate hornpipe; the lovers sing faux ballads, Dorie sings a faux lullaby, and the children don't sing at all. The sets are minimal. So is the orchestra, but we used two pianos instead.

I was Dorie Davis, and I never got past the absurdity of it. She is winsome and lissome, and I looked like someone's matronly Jewish aunt, especially in the heavy poplin turquoise dress with leg-of-mutton sleeves that someone made for me. But damn it, I was the lead, so I pretended I was desirable. I couldn't pretend that Dorie's songs sat comfortably in my voice; they were mostly in that troublesome middle range. But I had the part, so I sang it.

The surprise was that Miss Rigsbee was harsh and demanding. In the long evening rehearsals—too long for a small voice that tired easily—I couldn't do anything right. It's true that I didn't know how to move onstage and that my voice went in and out of focus. Still, she made me feel completely hopeless. Then she would smile her all-is-forgiven smile and I'd feel better. Warily. The rest of the cast, who were not training to be singers, sympathized with me; they'd always hated her. My piano teacher, Lucille, who was one of the accompanists, told me what I wanted to hear: "She's inhuman."

Dread set in. I was headed for humiliation. I knew how far from perfect I was, that I'd never get even halfway to perfection in this part. So I didn't feel I had the right to tell myself I was singing for Ann Drummond-Grant, who *was* perfection. Why would anyone pay to hear me? (Drummie actually drove herself half mad with perfectionism. A D'Oyly Carte colleague once saw her brought nearly to tears because she had a head cold and cracked one note—slightly—in an otherwise unblemished performance.)

There were two performances of *The Lowland Sea*, both to full houses in the school auditorium. On the morning of the first, I got my period and a curt rejection letter from Oberlin Conservatory. Neither surprised me. I did what I had to do, and so did we all, and the shows went fine. Miss Pinnell was pleased and sent white chrysanthemums, which in Japan are used for funerals. My parents sent violets, remembering that I was mad for them.

There remained the small matter of college. Lucille Sack, whose own two children were older and out of the house, wanted me to go to school in a city other than Syracuse. She met me at the library to look through college catalogs, though, this being April, it was too late to apply to most schools. Michigan State looked promising; they accepted applications till July. Or maybe I could transfer to Oberlin in my sophomore year. "The back door lets you in too," said Lucille. I nodded numbly. I had to start all over again with this thing I didn't want to do.

"You're a very wicked girl for not having thought about this six months ago, you know," she said, leafing through one catalog after another. "You've been incredibly lucky so far. You've had lots of things just fall into your lap." (Wasn't that how life was supposed to happen?) "Of course it takes about ten years for the voice to mature, and you can't really say . . . from what I've heard of your voice, it's not one of the great voices of the century. I think you'll find a place in some sort of musical theater. A combination of the two, you know."

"I do like to perform."

"Marcia, you're a *ham*." This was said affectionately. Then: "Look. You've just got to stop all of *this* [pantomimed histrionics] and grow up. These things may be fine among children, but they have no place among professionals. Actually, you are grown up in all the important ways. Now you just have to stop the hysterics."

Whipped-up emotions were my calling card, but they were exhausting. And I loved Lucille. If she thought I should apply to other schools, I would. But my parents didn't appreciate her intervention and put a stop to it. Syracuse had accepted me, and Syracuse it would be. I feel sure that my mother, deprived of a college education, would have jumped at the chance to go there.

My father was philosophical about Oberlin. I'd had only two years of training, he said, and was up against kids with scads more. No. I was up against kids with better voices, better audition pieces, and better preparation. It's a safe bet that not one of the voice students accepted by Oberlin that year had been driven by the desire to please a dead singer.

Well, I'd failed and would have to make the best of my failure.

At nearly eighteen, despite what Lucille said, I wasn't grown up at all, though I expended enormous energy pretending I was. The one indication of maturity was my willingness to work at things I really cared about. I was ambitious to tackle a Soler fandango I'd heard Fred Marvin play, a showy piece that wasn't terribly hard but was very, very long. Lucille not only thought I could play it, she programmed it on her student recital. So I had to memorize it and make it work for an audience. I rode my bicycle to the house of every friend with a piano and made them sit through it repeatedly so I could ferret out the trouble spots. The preparation paid off; the fandango was the hit of the night.

It's strange, now I think of it, that I never *sang* for my friends. But what good would it have done? If anyone had told me my singing was wonderful, I wouldn't have believed them, and if there were trouble spots, I wouldn't have known how to fix them. Maybe I was waiting for a solid vocal technique to "just fall into my lap" as the fruit of my earnest labors. Or maybe I didn't want to think about it.

When June came, Miss Rigsbee—once more the friend and benefactor—asked me to sing at graduation. Miss Pinnell and I chose two especially artsy songs that the audience was guaranteed not to relate to. My accompanists were a talented student pianist and a crying baby somewhere in the back of the restless, sweaty crowd.

Afterward, still in my fussy long dress, I ran over to Thornden Park to catch the end of the "alternative" graduation ceremony organized by Ray and his hippie-intellectual friends.

The gathering was small. The men were unshaven, and every-one wore not-recently-washed jeans. But Ray had somehow managed to book the legendary Delta Blues singer Son House, and I got to hear him. I dearly wish I'd known how to listen to him then, because he was the best thing about the day.

28

"LIKE *THIS*, DEAR."

SEVERAL PREDICTABLE THINGS HAPPENED that summer. Lisa and I got so competitive over Fred Marvin—a situation made worse by our pretending it didn't exist—that we became unable to stand each other. I left the yard work to her; Ernst was doing a lot of it anyway. And by that time, Fred was relying on us for other tasks. When he needed two hundred envelopes addressed for a promotional mailing, I was only too grateful to be asked. He rewarded me with the score of Soler's *Salve Regina*, which suited my voice. I learned it but had nowhere to sing it. Then Lisa won a local competition, and he gave her a recording, otherwise unobtainable, of himself playing Schubert. I refused to listen to it until he gave me a copy, but he never did.

After some weeks, Lucille Sack finally told me what I had refused to see: Fred and Ernst were a couple. It wasn't exactly a secret, but at that time and place, people didn't flaunt such things. They'd been together eleven years, having met at the Abbey of Saint Florian in Austria, where each had traveled to visit the grave of the composer Anton Bruckner. I didn't know that part of their story, but it explains why their nervous, elegant Shetland sheepdog was called Florian.

The news was more or less a relief—of course they were a couple!—but it caught me off guard. I hadn't yet been to music school, where all the really interesting men were gay; my gay classmates at Nottingham were closeted. This was around the time of the Stonewall Riots, more than a decade before AIDS. I went to school with some beautiful men who didn't survive the eighties.

I borrowed several library books about homosexuality. Most of what I read was not helpful. Mothers were largely at fault. Or maybe it was fathers. Either way, it was a perversion (or *inversion*, if you were British), and there was a lot of it in the world. I didn't think Fred and Ernst were perverts. Nor would I stop loving Fred, especially after hearing him play Beethoven's Opus 110 in recital. You never forget the man who awakens you to *that*.

Here I need to talk about piano technique a bit, because it was a hot issue at the school I was about to enter, and Fred was at the center of it. One of his teachers had been the great Chilean pianist Claudio Arrau, and it was Arrau's method that he taught. His insistence on doing so was dividing the piano students and faculty at SU into bitter factions. I hadn't known that piano technique could be divisive, but I could see why Arrau's was. Instead of articulating notes with your fingers, you relaxed your hands and rotated your wrists from side to side, letting your arms carry your fingers up and down the keyboard. It looked a little prissy. But it used the strength of the arms, shoulders, and back to—ideally—create a big, singing sound.

Lucille Sack encouraged wrist rotation, and I saw the sense of it. A modern grand piano is an eight-hundred-pound behemoth with metal strings under enormous tension. You need to put your whole body into it to make it sing. You also need fingers of steel. The day Fred accepted Lisa as a student, he had Lucille start her on Isidor Philipp's *Exercises for the Independence of the Fingers*, a whole book of particularly dreary knuckle-busters. Lisa entered them as one might enter a temple, though her fingers were already strong.

Had I been a better friend to Lisa that summer, I might have been more sensitive to what she was about to go through. It's one thing to be a talented high school piano student, and quite another to enter the studio of a serious concert artist, especially one who never forgets how serious he is. Fred was the tiresome sort of teacher who stops you after you play a single phrase—even a single note—and makes you go back to the beginning, over and over. Some of his students recall this form of torture almost gratefully, as a first experience of being held to a higher standard. I think it merely slaps the confidence out of you.

Fred's style of teaching must have been devastating for Lisa. All her hard work was being negated; she was being asked to start over and play his way. He was known for showing students how it was done. "Like *this*, dear," he'd say—and with those words, music became something to mimic rather than something that flowed through you. But submitting to Fred's version of the Arrau technique was the price of admission to his good graces.

There were many who saw Fred's teaching as rigid and wrongheaded. I've never heard such sniping as I heard that year from pianists who thought they knew better. But in music school, I soon learned, there were snipers everywhere.

29

SHALIMAR AND POT

When I started at Syracuse University in the fall of 1971, its once-renowned music school had slid far downhill. It was a time of campus unrest, and while the general student body protested Nixon and Vietnam, the music students rose up against their own dean. The university had run up a large deficit, and there wasn't enough money to go around. The faculty fought over these shrinking resources, and as always in academia, the fights got nastier as the budget got smaller.

Just as I arrived, the beleaguered dean resigned. The music school was merged with the art and drama schools in a new entity called the College of Visual and Performing Arts. Strictly a financial move and, yes, a bad idea. There was no crossover between the art and music schools—as Lucille Sack put it, "there are no sculptors studying music theory." But the art students needed space; they took over some of the choice music studios in Crouse College.

Worse, the administration had stopped making any effort to recruit talented music students. Such efforts cost money. There were a few promising freshmen who had come to study with the better-known teachers—Fred, for example, or the distinguished soprano Helen Boatwright. But many of my new classmates weren't gifted enough or advanced enough to aspire to a music career. I found myself paddling in a pool of mediocrity: pianists who couldn't play, singers who couldn't sing, and a composer who, I swear to God, bragged about being tone-deaf. I was afraid I belonged among these people. It was my punishment for not being good enough.

I had to pretend otherwise. I'd gotten myself into this situation, wagered my future on it. I had to shine. Shine at . . . what, exactly? It was a good thing I didn't aspire to sing opera, because there was no opera department. I knew I didn't want a degree in music education, though that would at least have been a way to make a living. In some part of my brain, the part where I'd known that Fred was gay and Ann Drummond-Grant had died, I knew that joining the D'Oyly Carte was probably not in the cards for an American girl who couldn't get her singing together. But I was pretending I could. I was outspoken, flamboyant, ostentatiously musical. I told myself I could put over a German art song better than any of my freshman classmates.

My voice, however, still had no reliable middle. At the first student convocation of the year, I stood on the stage of Crouse Auditorium, the same stage where Fred had played, and sang a Brahms song, "Von ewiger Liebe." It's a dramatic little scene between two young lovers. The boy fears the girl will be ashamed of him, and the girl swears their love is stronger than steel. I had no stage fright. I knew my voice would carry well in that live space. Which it did, until I got to the girl's declaration:

> *Eisen und Stahl, man schmiedet sie um,*
> *Unsere Liebe, wer wandelt sie um?*
>
> [Iron and steel can be reforged,/ but our love—who will change it?]

The word *Eisen* fell squarely in the break between registers, where I couldn't produce a full tone. The note quavered; the bottom fell out of it. Every other note in the song was fine. People congratulated me on my performance, but I knew better. That one note was proof I wasn't a singer.

Reader, I wasn't as bad as that. But I had an all-or-nothing mentality. That one bad note killed the performance for me. I've never forgotten it.

Did it occur to me to look for another teacher? It did not. I convinced myself that there'd been enough improvement in my singing to justify sticking with Miss Pinnell. Our working relationship was the only holdover from my high school life. Everything else was new and disorienting.

Having had my own large bedroom, I was now sharing a small cinderblock room in a dorm. I'd brought my G&S records, unwilling to part from them, but had no privacy to listen to them. Rock music familiar to everyone but me poured out of the other rooms; the whole floor smelled of Shalimar and pot. Every afternoon, an execrable marching band practiced for two hours in a field outside my window. There were thousands of students at SU, all (it seemed to me) obsessed with parties and football.

My first roommate, a Long Island girl as social as I was serious, didn't last a day. We took one look at each other and knew it wouldn't work. She had a friend she wanted to room with, so I took the friend's assigned roommate, who was short and stout and introduced herself by saying, "I'm a stumpy"—meaning she was enrolled at the College of Forestry. The stumpy was having a tough time adjusting, so our conversations consisted mostly of her arias of self-pity.

I did my own share of wallowing that first semester, silently, into my notebook. Never had I been so lost and unhappy. It seemed to me I stood out as the emotive girl who didn't belong anywhere and therefore didn't exist. I haunted the halls of Crouse like a buxom wraith, hoping Fred Marvin would walk by. I wasn't in love with him anymore, but he was all I had, and the mere sight of him released a flood of endorphins that felt like joy.

Fred, however, gave me the cold shoulder. If he saw me, he'd pretend he was looking for someone else. It was deliberate, uncalled for. Did he think I wasn't on his side? He had enemies. George Papastavrou, head of the piano faculty, had circulated a petition demanding that Fred be denied tenure. There was a Marvin camp and a Papastavrou camp, each professing elaborate disdain for the other, like Baptists and Anabaptists. The pianos themselves were at odds: two concert grands sat on the stage in Crouse Auditorium, one marked "M" and the other marked "P."

Fred soon rewarmed to me as mysteriously as he'd gone cold. I stood up for him stoutly, though I'd begun to notice the harrowing memory slips that plagued his performances. In a piece he knew perfectly well, he'd suddenly go blank and start faking his way through, sometimes badly; I'd listen with my heart in my mouth. Every pianist has memory slips, but Fred's were pathological.

He was still my hero. After a famous pianist gave a recital downtown, one of Papastavrou's grad students asked me how I'd liked the concert. "The Chopin was all right," I sniffed, "but Marvin would have played it better." Papa's student pounced. "Listen, you're a bright kid," he said. "Why are you shutting yourself in a corner? Marvin's such a charlatan! He's got you right under his thumb, and there are so many pianists so much better than he is!" I wouldn't hear it. Fred, imperfect though he was, was not a charlatan. But in that charged environment, words like *charlatan* were flung.

30

THE TWINS

I HAD A NEW PIANO TEACHER—as a voice major, I was required to minor in piano—and this teacher was a concert pianist with a promising international career. Richard Contiguglia and his twin brother, John, were duo pianists, meaning they specialized in the repertoire for four hands. Though they played with major orchestras and had made prizewinning recordings, they were underlings at Crouse, sharing one teaching job, one tiny salary, one apartment, and one (used) Volkswagen beetle. And they were stuck teaching piano minors like me.

Thanks to Lucille Sack, I was better than the average piano minor, and Richard, finding me worth his attention, assigned pieces that challenged me. Actually they were too difficult, but I liked that. It meant I could shut myself in one of the decrepit basement practice rooms at Crouse and pound away for hours without having to think about singing or the ambient mediocrity or my own deepening despair. I toyed with the idea of transferring my affections to Richard, who was closer to my age than Fred, a mere thirty-four. I wasn't really attracted to him, but I would soon learn that attraction could be manufactured in a pinch.

More than usual that fall and winter, I was plagued by colds and sore throats that led to laryngitis. There was always some physical reason I couldn't or shouldn't sing. Not only was I not improving, I seemed to be going backward.

There are only so many times you can fling yourself against the same wall, and I was hitting multiple walls. Vocal technique was a wall. So was Fred. So, increasingly, was Richard. I began to think there was something wrong with me. Why did I keep falling for unavailable men? Here, for once, Lucille Sack was not helpful. She'd read Freud, and as far as she was concerned, I had some kind of father complex. I thought she meant I was sexually attracted to my father, and this idea upset me deeply. My father represented another wall, the one I built around my emotions to keep him from feeding on them. Which I suppose was a complex of a sort.

Both my parents were walled off in their separate ways. My father was sphinxlike, guardian of his own riddles. Mother hid what feelings she had behind a barricade of brusque annoyance. They were the last people I would have confided in now, when I was failing so appallingly at the course I'd insisted on.

As for unavailable men—well, it was music school. The only men at Crouse who were guaranteed to be straight were the brass players. The rest might or might not be straight, but either way, they were complicated. Like me. It seems to me now that I was putting off sex until I was good and ready for it. But in the moment, I felt abnormal and ashamed.

In the middle of that average Syracuse winter—relentlessly snowy, slushy, dark—I lost it. Lost the way, the truth, the light. Thought about losing the life. A Nottingham classmate of mine had killed herself at the beginning of the school year. I'd known Anita most of my life. She was the smart one in every subject, the one who scored a hundred on science tests and blew the curve for the rest of us. She was the capable pianist who accompanied me at graduation, the nice girl with the slight overbite who was just coming into her beauty. Anita had been accepted at a good college but somehow didn't fare well; she wound up attending SU and living at home. One morning, her mother found her dead of a sleeping-pill overdose. Something had gotten to her, and she'd slipped away. Her absence was unfathomable to me. But I was beginning to understand how she'd lost her bearings, how it felt to be lost.

Perhaps she hadn't believed she would succeed at suicide. Perhaps it had been easier than she thought. I began to see how it could be easy to cross that border and think you wouldn't be missed, or that your absence wouldn't matter. It was natural to consider this, and the naturalness frightened me.

It's possible that if I'd undergone a similar crisis at Oberlin, an isolated place where no one knew me, I might not have come through it. But I was on home ground, and as long as I could put pen to paper, even if it produced drivel, I could touch a voice that was discernibly mine—acid, secret, wide awake. I was writing for myself, so I could say anything. I allowed myself to consider suicide and saw that it wasn't possible. My body could die, but I was more than a body. I felt a presence, a larger self, that couldn't be dispatched with razors or pills. The larger self had to be answered to, just as Ann Drummond-Grant, the lady of my notebooks, had to be answered to. I was a mess. All I could do was scribble and weep. But it mattered that I was alive.

I scribbled at Lucille Sack's house. She and her husband, Milt, had gone off on a winter vacation and left me a key. The idea was that I could practice, but I spent whole afternoons sitting at her kitchen table in my winter coat—she'd said to turn up the heat, but I thought that would be expensive. Anyhow, the sun streamed in. And the radio, tuned to the local classical station, provided a certain warmth. One of Fred's recordings popped up amid the Tchaikovsky and Vaughan Williams.

(I noted, "That Schubert Adagio is less boring than I remembered.") I finished a cryptic crossword Lucille had started in *New York* magazine. It was a comfort. So was the white kitchen wall by the table, where she'd written, in pencil, in her clear large hand, the phone numbers of people she regularly called, including me.

31

EDINBURGH, 1933

ANN DRUMMOND-GRANT WAS NEARLY twenty-nine when she finally left home, abandoning her small, straitlaced city to gain an entire world.

Her sister, Agnes, was married in July 1933 at the Presbyterian church where Drummie had been soprano soloist. Drummie was there, most likely as maid of honor. But by then, she'd been a chorister with the D'Oyly Carte Company for five months, during which time the company had performed in Newcastle, Sheffield, Manchester, Leeds, Leicester, Cambridge, Blackpool, and Dublin. When you joined the D'Oyly Carte, your home was an unending series of dressing rooms, stages, and boarding houses, all drafty. The operas—ten, in repertory—were the only constant.

The company played Edinburgh every two or three years, so Drummie would have known it well and, I'm guessing, itched to audition. Agnes's engagement seems to have freed her to do so, most likely during the company's Edinburgh stint in March 1933. Many in the ladies' chorus auditioned as sweet young things just out of music school. Drummie was older, but this worked in her favor. She had the sort of big soprano voice that takes time to mature. (It's like having a car with a powerful engine: it's not enough to own the thing; you have to learn how to handle it.) And because she had some stage experience, she might have found it less intimidating to learn ten operas at once. Though I doubt it.

Drummie was significantly taller than the average chorister. The staging, preserved largely intact from Gilbert's time, generally involved the women standing in semicircular rows, so she would have stuck out, even wearing flats. But that voice! The musical director—Isidore Godfrey, her future husband—must have heard it and hired her on the spot, height be damned. This was someone who could one day sing principal soprano roles. In the company's 1936 recording of *The Mikado*, I'm willing to swear I can discern Drummie's voice in the ladies' chorus. It's quite a distinctive voice, and though she blends beautifully as a chorister should, her vibrato is clear as day.

It was no small achievement to become part of the well-oiled machine that was the D'Oyly Carte. Cynthia Morey, a principal soprano who went through the process in 1951 (and was onstage during Drummie's above-mentioned brassiere mishap in *Iolanthe*), describes it in her indispensable memoir *Inclined to Dance and Sing*. First, she says, you were drilled in the choral parts for hours, days, weeks on end—not just to learn the notes, but to acquire the perfect pellucid diction the company was famous for. Morey was drilled by Maude Evans, who was then in her eighties and had worked with Gilbert himself.

Next, you were measured and fitted for costumes, including shoes, that had been worn by someone else. You were fitted with heavy wigs that were attached to the forehead with spirit gum. D'Oyly Carte costumes allowed no opportunities for immodesty. Morey's outfit for *Trial By Jury*, in which she sang the opening chorus and sat silently for the rest of the show, consisted of "black cotton stockings, elastic-sided boots, long white lace-trimmed drawers, a red flannel petticoat, a calico crinoline stiffened with whalebone hoops, a cotton petticoat, a woolen skirt and jacket, a bonnet and muff." Full Victorian regalia, in other words, and no fun in warm weather. The authentic kimono for *The Mikado* had long silk bloomers underneath and two long white tapes hanging in front—"virginity strings"— that had to be tied in a bow at all times.

After their fittings, new choristers were trained in their myriad stage moves and little dance steps. Drummie would have learned bowing, simpering, and shuffling for *The Mikado*, lovesick swooning for *Patience*, fairylike tripping for *Iolanthe*, a hornpipe for *Pinafore*, and a cachucha for *The Gondoliers*. Two other choristers joined at the same time she did. The three of them would have done a lot of drilling before setting foot onstage with the rest of the cast.

Joining the company in Edinburgh in the middle of a run—as opposed to London, where the costumers and regular rehearsal rooms were located—must have felt like working without a net. But the D'Oyly Carte was a true family: the work was relentless and exacting, and the only way to ensure a good performance every time was for everyone to look out for everyone else.

Even though they had contracts, members of the company were always made to feel they were on probation. If they were promoted to principal roles, it was "for the time being" or "until further notice." Salaries were small, and everyone had to pay their own expenses: food, lodging, transportation, makeup. But the D'Oyly Carte was unusual in that it offered steady, year-round work with a regular paycheck and a devoted audience. For struggling freelance artists who made the cut, it was a kind of nirvana.

I think—I *think*—I would have adored it till I couldn't stand it anymore. Drummie seems never to have stopped adoring it.

At the end of her first season, one of her fellow choristers left the company to marry a neurologist. Unless you married within the company (something that was not actively encouraged), gaining a husband often meant losing a career. This particular chorister received a parting gift that left no doubt about her future: a leather-bound cookbook filled with handwritten recipes from her colleagues.

Drummie contributed her recipe for scones—the classic Edinburgh kind, made without sugar. Those scones are plain and a bit grim; I think she must have baked them a thousand times. In the cook's shorthand that was the norm in those days, when women were assumed to have learned the basics from their mothers, Drummie calls for a piece of butter "the size of an egg" (a quarter of a cup, it turns out) and "sufficient milk to make a nice, soft consistency," however much that is. She doesn't say how to work the dough or shape the scones, or specify a cooking time, trusting that the bride will know all that. "Here," she seems to be saying, "*you* bake these now. I'm starting my *real* life."

32

OUR BODIES, OURSELVES, 1972

THE SECOND SEMESTER OF MY FRESHMAN YEAR was marginally less rocky than the first. I was half aware I was looking for an identity: if I wasn't shaping up as the singer I aspired to be, who was I? I left it to those around me to decide, putting myself out for remodeling as one might solicit bids from contractors. Who did *they* think I was?

I had a new roommate, having managed to ditch the stumpy. Jeannie was from a beach town at the far end of Long Island, a summer enclave for the rich. Her family was merely well-to-do—her father was a dentist—but she moved through the world with a quiet confidence that spoke of wealth to me. She was Irish on both sides, a cool blonde with four red-headed younger brothers. When I first met her, she was a student of nursing and mad for Jesus, though she never visited that ardor on me. I was aware only that she was determined to be kind and generous: she not only put up with me, she loved me. It can't have been easy, skittish and secretive as I was. I was grateful she thought my friendship worth having.

She was the first person I met who called herself a feminist, a word I didn't know I needed to know. Her circle of friends owned copies of *Our Bodies, Ourselves* and talked comfortably about their vaginas. They referred to themselves as women, not girls. I thought this was pretentious until I realized it was simply a fact. We *were* women. I'd never called myself that or thought about what it meant. In Jeannie's circle, it meant having the right to be listened to and taken seriously. And the right to sexual pleasure, with or without a man. I could believe in the second, but not the first.

Her friends liked going braless and encouraged me to try it. So I did, once, borrowing Jeannie's embroidered Mexican peasant blouse for the occasion. The coarse-woven cotton rubbed my nipples raw, and my bouncing breasts seemed to issue an invitation I didn't intend.

Jeannie herself was short and curvy. She thought she ought to be thinner—every girl with flesh thought that—but had complete faith in her own attractiveness. Men adored her, probably because she cared about them as people, something I hadn't learned to do. Like me, she was a virgin. Like me, she wanted capital-L Love. Unlike me, she was on her way to understanding what that was. I felt comfortable with her male friends but couldn't see them romantically, probably because they were my own age and heterosexual. Yet I thought it fine and charming to tease and denigrate them. They were nice about it.

Jeannie encouraged my nascent romantic interest in my piano teacher, Richard, though I wasn't sure this interest was a good or viable idea. It intrigued me to think I might learn a few feminine wiles from her, being basically wile-free. She told me Richard would love my long hair, which my mother hated. (I'd refused to cut it for several years. It was dark blonde, thick and straight, and hung like a curtain.) Actually Jeannie had no idea what Richard would love, and neither did I. Richard was inscrutable. Doubly inscrutable when you factored in John, his identical twin. Living together, practicing together, performing together, they seemed a self-contained universe of two.

Being twins gave them an edge in the four-hand piano repertoire, where two must literally play as one. Even seated on
opposite sides of a stage at separate grand pianos, Richard and
John were never out of sync. What disagreements they had
were hashed out in practice; in performance, they were of one
musical mind. Lucille Sack said, "Those boys have an absolutely
superb ensemble, the best I've heard." She always called them
"the boys," though they were fast approaching middle age.

There *was* a boyishness about them. They dressed like
college kids and treated their more dedicated students as
friends—as grownups—rather than keeping a professorial distance. They were local boys (men!) who had won scholarships
to Yale, after which they'd studied in London with the legendary pianist Myra Hess, who taught them how to produce a
large, ringing sound—the difference between playing in a living room and projecting from a concert stage.

Their playing was bigger and more athletic than Fred's; both
spent serious time at the gym maintaining their upper-body
strength. I would hear Richard (or was it John?) practicing his
half of one of the big bravura pieces they specialized in—Liszt's
transcription of Beethoven's 9th Symphony, or Bartok's fiend-
ishly difficult Suite for Two Pianos—in their basement studio
at Crouse, attacking tough passages over and over, the notes
resounding up and down the hallway.

Richard was not, for a dozen readily apparent reasons, boyfriend material, and I would never have viewed him as such if
I hadn't been so desperate to be in love. He valued my opinion
and took me seriously as a musician—that is, he liked me—and
Jeannie seemed to think he could be won by an attractive, loving woman who encouraged him to pour out his heart. I was
game. I showed up for lessons in Jeannie's flowing dresses and
my own flowing hair, trailing some fragrance I deemed both
innocent and sexy (Blue Grass, or Love's Baby Soft Lemon

Fresh Cologne), willing myself to be adorable. None of it mattered. What mattered was that I practiced like mad, wrestling with large pieces that were more than a shade too difficult for me: a Beethoven sonata; a Schumann suite; a Bach fugue. Nothing matched the exhilaration of working on these pieces, getting better at them and bringing them in triumph to Richard, who applauded my progress while showing me how much more work I had to do.

I contrived without much success to feel physically attracted to him. Auburn-haired, neither tall nor short, he (John, too) was good-looking in a way that might have been Italian or Jewish. I admired his hands with their long, elegant fingers—those being what I noticed at my lessons when he demonstrated points of technique. But attraction, for me, always began with words: I lost interest in many a good-looking man the minute he opened his mouth. My way of wooing Richard was through conversation. We talked and talked.

As for getting him to pour out his heart, I did try. But he was perfectly comfortable in the shell Jeannie thought he needed to be coaxed out of. I, however, began to believe I was in love with him—probably because I revealed my own feelings while trying to make him reveal his. I wasn't accustomed to sharing feelings. My go-to romantic strategy was to aim a stream of madcap brilliance at someone who wasn't paying attention. If Richard was falling for me, he had an odd way of showing it, drawing back instinctively if I so much as touched his arm. His interest in me was strictly musical.

He and John were good teachers, and we-their-students formed a kind of benign cult. Some of us had crushes on one or the other of them, but the crushes were a byproduct of the intensity of studying music. The Contiguglias had their students perform at every opportunity, guiding them toward careers as working musicians—if not as solo pianists, as accompanists or coaches. I don't think this was happening anywhere else in the piano department.

It certainly wasn't the norm in the voice department, where Miss Pinnell and her colleague Frank Hakanson nurtured crop after crop of singers who sounded like talented amateurs and wound up teaching high school students or doing something else entirely. There was just one teacher whose students stood a chance of amounting to something: Helen Boatwright, the famous lyric soprano. I didn't even think of approaching her. Lucille Sack had dismissed that idea early on by saying, "Helen's a good teacher for students who already have a solid technique." Not me, in other words.

33

SHORTBREAD AND SCHUBERT

THE ONE FORMATIVE SINGING EXPERIENCE I had at Crouse was the visit of Hermann Reutter, a German composer and accompanist who gave master classes in lieder interpretation. A master he was, both in vocal technique and in conveying the nuances of the German art song. He was seventy-two, a papa bear of a man, very much the éminence but also very approachable. I immediately felt comfortable with him. I wasn't the worst singer who sang for him; among the undergraduates, the bar was not high. I sang a Schumann song, "Mondnacht," about a clear moonlit night so beautiful it makes the soul spread its wings "as though it were flying home." It's one of those gorgeous songs that's a privilege to sing, with a long, sustained line that must be spun with quiet intensity.

When I finished, he said, much to my surprise, "Nice voice, very nice voice." And then proceeded to tell me, gently, in a thick German accent, what was maybe not so nice. My diaphragm, he said, was "very bad." My *ah* vowel was not well produced, and I wasn't using my lips, tongue, or teeth to place the sound. On the spot, he woke me up to thinking about vowels and consonants in a way that helped enormously. But what was I supposed to do about that diaphragm, the engine of everything? His answer: "Swim! Hours and hours a day—it's the only way! See, here, it has to be like this. . . ."

Inevitably, he placed my hand against his abdomen to demonstrate. "It's not force, you see, it's a muscle, and it must be developed."

Once more I felt a strong diaphragm in action, and once more I was clueless about what it was doing. Herr Reutter was right about swimming. If I'd known how to swim properly and been able to devote significant energy to it, I would have built those crucial muscles. But I wouldn't have known how to use them.

I did eventually learn what breath support was, but not for another sixteen years. Attempting one last blessed time to learn to sing at age thirty-five, I began lessons with a teacher named Sam Sakarian who knew what he was doing. Sam got me into the habit of drawing my diaphragm inward as I sang. I didn't know why I did it, or whether it had any effect. A few months in, I caught a streaming cold that came with a headful of snot. As I blew my nose (and blew, and blew), I reflexively pulled my diaphragm in. Lo! That inward motion pushed the snot right out of my head. At long last I made the physical connection: the diaphragm pushes the breath, and the breath pushes the snot . . . and the sound! For the first time in my life, I was powering my voice from the right place. After a few more months, I could feel my abdominal muscles engage as the diaphragm pulled in. I had a singer's firm gut. Like Herr Reutter's. Like Miss Pinnell's.

That was my Helen Keller moment—like the moment when Keller, as a deaf-blind six-year-old, made the revelatory connection between water being pumped over one hand and the word w-a-t-e-r being spelled into the other. She gained access to language; I gained access to singing. If I'd gained it earlier, my life might have been different. But when Herr Reutter tried to explain breath support to me, I was ill-equipped to understand him. I could only listen in frustration as others sang with a full, grownup sound when I couldn't.

One singer in Herr Reutter's master class, a grad student named Susan, had such a sound. Her creamy soprano would have made me jealous if I hadn't liked her so much. Susan was English, deeply musical, and blind. She was verbal and quick-witted (like me) and made killer shortbread she was happy to share. She even knew a little G&S. We were pals.

Susan had come to Syracuse to study with Helen Boatwright but had found her unnervingly temperamental. Helen was known for yelling at students during lessons and hugging them afterward, a form of tough love that would have unnerved me too. That year she was even more volatile because of the politics at Crouse. She may have been a star in the music world, but she felt disrespected by the university. Susan told me Helen was prone to outbursts of fury over this—"Don't they know who I *am?*"—and required a good deal of comforting.

This was not what Susan wanted in her lessons. So she left Helen and went to study with Frank Hakanson. None of the other voice students could believe this. It was a privilege—and a career booster—to study with Helen, who was famed for the purity of her singing and the depth of her musicianship. I'd heard her sing thorny twentieth-century works (Schoenberg's *Erwartung*, Hindemith's *Das Marienleben*) with the same radiant ease she displayed in Bach and Mozart. Frank Hakanson, on the other hand, was famed for knowing precious little about teaching vocal technique. ("Better a hacking cough," said Lucille.) But he didn't throw tantrums, and that mattered to Susan, who was finding very little to love at SU.

Susan didn't have a guide dog—she didn't like dogs— but was adept with her white cane. She knew her way to and from the graduate residence where she invited me for that shortbread. But this was a Syracuse winter. The sidewalks were treacherous with ice and blowing snow; even on sunny days, the street corners were ankle deep in slush. She found Crouse a depressing place, with too much mediocrity and too little collegiality. There was another blind student, an unhinged organ major named Frank, who became obsessed with Susan and went around calling her name; we had to shield her from him. The year and a half she spent getting her master's degree was one long slog. Herr Reutter's visit was the only bright spot.

Susan was working on Schubert's cycle *Die schöne Müllerin* for her recital in May. When she sang the first song for Herr Reutter, he made her sing the next one, and the next: this was clearly no student, but an artist with something to say. By the time they'd gone through ten of the twenty songs, he said, "I have to play these for you," and it was decided. She would give the recital now, in February, with Herr Reutter at the keyboard. For Susan, there was no question about feeling ready. Here was a chance to be coached by a master of the lieder repertoire.

I was drafted as page turner. Herr Reutter didn't really need a page turner. Most of the songs were just one or two pages long, and he already knew the music. But he liked me, bad diaphragm and all. So for the next scant week, I got to be there at rehearsals, soaking up Herr Reutter's insights as the two of them went deeper and deeper into the songs. It was what I needed. Schubert's music always goes where it hurts, and right then it was the only thing shoring me up.

I longed to sing those songs. They were within my range. I had no trouble learning the notes or enunciating the German. I felt the emotions of the poor miller who gets ditched by the girl of his dreams (she wants someone manlier) and flings himself into the mill stream. But my voice, next to Susan's, was thin and patchy. I had to distort some vowels to make them sound at all. Her voice, though not large, was smooth from top to bottom, readily able to do whatever Schubert asked. She was three years older than me and light years ahead.

It was enough that week to be near the music, and to be part of the odd trio we made trooping across the snow-covered campus, Susan on Herr Reutter's arm. I amused him, or perhaps reminded him of someone. For whatever reason, it was clear we all delighted each other.

Susan's recital was not well attended, having been scheduled at the last minute. Those who came were glad they did. It was music making of a high order, and it carried us far away from that poisoned place. Miss Pinnell came backstage with tears in her eyes. I'd never seen her that way.

Herr Reutter left the next day. The parting was hard. He impulsively handed me a little packet of cookies. "You are tired." (I was always complaining about being tired, and he was always chaffing me about it.) "These will help you wake up, maybe." Then he said, out of nowhere, "I hope you find the right man. He will come soon."

"He" didn't, of course, but those were exactly the right words.

34

THE SORROWFUL MONK

A WEEK BEFORE HERR REUTTER'S arrival on campus, I'd done a star turn of my own, one that didn't involve singing. Richard Contiguglia, seeing that I was a dramatic sort (he could hardly have missed it), decided I would be perfect for a Liszt narration-with-piano called *Der traurige Mönch*—The Sorrowful Monk. Such recitations, called melodramas, were peculiarly nineteenth-century entertainments. If you couldn't sing at a musical soiree, you might profitably declaim at one.

What's extraordinary about this melodrama, from 1860, is that Liszt uses a whole-tone scale, the harmonically ambiguous sonority that, decades later, became Debussy's trademark. There's scarcely a major or minor chord in the piece. The effect is mysterious and mournful, befitting this tale of a knight ambushed by a spectral monk whose eyes express all the sorrows of the world.

It was right up my alley.

I could have declaimed the piece in German, but since Richard wanted it performed at a student convocation, I offered to do an English translation. I sat down with my first-year German teacher to get the literal meaning of the text, then put it into its proper meter—not too difficult for a girl with a good ear who'd spent so much time with Gilbert and Sullivan.

My pianist, Carol, was another student of Richard's, far more advanced than I. She, too, had a crush on him, but we weren't about to let that get in the way of the performance. Far better that we should walk onstage that Thursday morning with the proper gravitas—or rather, that she should walk onstage, and that I should follow as she played the intro, head bowed, wearing a long, hooded black cape. When I lifted my face, it was painted stark white with black eyeliner and mascara. And then I intoned the text in my best stentorian diction, letting the voice resonate in my chest, channeling all the contraltos of the D'Oyly Carte.

The poor knight! He and his little horse lose their way at dusk and take shelter in an ancient gray tower . . . where, in the middle of the night, they are awakened by a blinding light and the hideous apparition of the monk with the fatal sorrow in his eyes. Fatal because after seeing it, horse and rider are lost to the world. Before another sunset, they stroll aimlessly into the nearest lake. (There would seem to be a lot of drowning in German Romantic poetry.)

The audience didn't know what hit it. There was a gulp of silence, then large applause. I think this was mostly due to the surprise factor; no one had seen or heard anything like it. But I have to say I was good. Liberated from worry about vocal technique, I really put the piece across. People who had little to say about my singing went out of their way to praise my dramatic presence. Fred immediately booked me to declaim it at one of his soirees, from the balcony, in German, with him at the piano. Everyone there acted like a star was born.

Richard and John both became convinced that my true calling was as an actress. They began steering me, not subtly, toward a double major in music and drama and arranged for me to meet with the head of the drama school to find out what this might entail. And I went—because I was fine with letting them tell me who I was. Because I was sick of not being good at singing and could fairly easily pump up an ambition to be an actress. How hard could acting be?

Never mind that there was no such thing as a double major in music and drama at SU. There was a musical theater program, but I didn't want that—I wanted to sing Gilbert and Sullivan, not belt out Broadway tunes. I didn't understand that proper vocal training would have enabled me to do both.

I told Miss Pinnell that while I apparently didn't have the talent to be a classical singer, I had a gift for acting, so I would focus on that.

"You do have a great talent there," said Miss Pinnell, "and I've always been particularly impressed with your speaking voice, the way it carries on a stage. I'm just *waiting* for some of that depth to show up in your singing voice. It must be there *somewhere*."

Oh. She was *waiting* for it. It wasn't about to show up on its own, especially now that I was allowing myself still more distraction from practicing singing. I had to pretend I cared about observing people, the better to become the actress I now believed I was. I was so wedded to my own theatricality that I didn't realize I was actually a flaming introvert.

Toward the end of the semester, Richard broke the news that he and John were leaving SU. They'd asked for a raise and been told there was no money, so they couldn't see a reason for staying. Their concert career was taking off, and they wanted to live in Europe. I could hardly blame them.

By the terms of our unspoken agreement, Richard and I had no relationship other than that of professor and student. We were friends, but it was a friendship once removed: he could remove himself whenever he liked. So I couldn't rightly say he was leaving me. He was just leaving. I had to adjust to the idea that he and John would be gone from my life.

As it happened, they stayed in Syracuse another six months. I studied privately with Richard over the summer, and we were close in our disembodied fashion: I beguiled him with clever talk while he studiously avoided romantic openings. The highlight was his assigning me a large piece by Liszt, "Saint Francis of Assisi Preaching to the Birds." It was flashy and soulful, with lots of twittering; I could just manage it. I very much liked the idea of Saint Francis, to whom everything and everyone—the sun, the moon, animals, poverty—was a brother or sister. Francis had, I thought, a radical way of embracing life: it was mystical, it was delirious, it made sense to me.

I lived at home that summer, riding my bike over the hills to Crouse every day so I could practice in the Contiguglias' studio, lacking a decent piano of my own. Crouse was a far better place without people in it. Miss Pinnell was away, so I didn't have to think about singing. And now that Richard was leaving the country, I wasn't sure about acting either. All I wanted was to be alone in a room with a piano.

I never told Richard about Ann Drummond-Grant. I never spoke her name to a living soul. She was my patron saint, whose life I was building my life on. I still adored her, even as I was being carried further and further from my dream of joining the D'Oyly Carte.

35

THE SORROWFUL
SOPRANO, 1935-1938

Ann Drummond-Grant was thirty-one when she became a D'Oyly Carte principal soprano. There are two kinds of soprano roles in Gilbert and Sullivan: those that can be sung by a light lyric voice, and those that call for more vocal heft. Drummie sang the latter kind and sang them very well. But after two short years, she was banished for falling in love—like Iolanthe, come to think of it. So she didn't have those parts long enough to make them indelibly hers.

I've gathered ephemeral traces of her work in that decade: lovingly preserved programs from regional theaters, newspaper clippings, scraps of reviews. I also have publicity photos of her in costume, some of which are xeroxes—ghosts of photos— because that's what the company archivist was able to send me. Even those stark images say a lot.

For one thing, and I'm embarrassed to admit it was the first thing I noticed, she was slender. As a teenager, I would spend hours looking at photos of Drummie in the hoop-skirted con-tralto costumes of the fifties and wondering, was she fat? How fat *was* she? It was exactly the same conversation I regularly had with the mirror. If Drummie was heavy, it would be okay to be heavy. But I wanted her thin, because thin was better. As it turns out, she was positively svelte.

Even at her thinnest, she was made for singing, built like a Valkyrie, with strong shoulders and an expansive chest. She had broad cheeks—good sinus cavities make for good resonance—and a rather thick neck, suitable to the large instrument it held. Corseted into form-fitting costumes and photographed from the front, she looked almost dainty, as Gilbert's sopranos were supposed to look. But she towered over some of her leading men and had to wear flats onstage.

Just how tall was she? Tony Joseph, author of that fine history of the D'Oyly Carte, got me the answer from the company archives: five feet, seven inches—not terribly tall by today's standards, but several inches taller than the average British woman of her day. She carried her height proudly and even wore heels. Though she put on some weight in middle age, she was never really heavy. She was exactly the right size and shape to play Gilbert's formidable, queenly contraltos.

The other thing these photos tell me is that, even when playing innocent young ladies, Drummie bore the mark of bitter experience. Always interested in the serious side—the "dramatic" side, as she put it—of any character, she projected a closely held sorrow, the sorrow that drew me to her in the first place. There's a shot of her as Josephine in *Pinafore*, unsmiling, eyes lifted, thinking stoic thoughts. Josephine does face a dilemma: she loves a poor sailor and agonizes about all she stands to lose if she marries him. That scene is a parody of grand opera, sung with a straight face because the situation is incredibly silly. The straight face, however, was Drummie's own.

Other photos corroborate this. In costume as the saucy, feisty Plaintiff in *Trial by Jury*, Drummie wears a musing, half-sad smile. As Patience, the lighthearted milkmaid, she looks awfully rueful about something. In full armor as Princess Ida, the flinty rebel who takes no guff from anyone, she seems utterly hopeless and alone—which is appropriate to the character for maybe five minutes of the opera.

There's a framed photo on my desk of Drummie as Elsie Maynard in *The Yeomen of the Guard*, sitting with her hands in her lap, looking numbly into some void—revealing, I've always thought, a fundamental aloneness. It's one of three studio portraits from a sitting in 1938. In the other two she's smiling and looking hopeful—in one, she's waving a tambourine. (Elsie is a street singer.) But even those smiles are not quite happy. The girl can't help it.

Yeomen is the opera where Gilbert and Sullivan determined to rise above their reputations as purveyors of comic frippery. The musical numbers are superb, some of their best. The drama works pretty well, too, though it's over-plotted and over-earnest—something that happens to Gilbert when he's avoiding being funny. It's set in the Tower of London in the sixteenth century. People say "forsooth"; someone fires an arquebus. The comic baritone is a court jester replete with cap and bells—an embittered funnyman, Gilbert's proxy. There are Beefeaters in doublets and ruffled collars. And there's going to be a beheading, any minute now, on Tower Green. The notable thing about the plot is that while the characters pair off at the end in true Gilbertian fashion, hardly anyone winds up happy. The jester actually *dies*. (The stage directions say he "falls insensible," but it's usually played as a heart attack.)

Elsie is in a serious bind. To afford medicine for her ailing mother, she's agreed to marry the prisoner who's about to be beheaded. (He wants to foil a would-be heir. Don't ask.) She sings an affecting aria about being a bride who'll be widowed in half an hour—and then the prisoner escapes, and her real troubles begin. Most sopranos playing Elsie, though, don't look like martyrs in training. Drummie does.

Mind you, the martyred look disappears when she's photographed in street clothes. I believe she was actually quite happy in the thirties. Her world was opening up. In 1934, a year after she joined the D'Oyly Carte as a chorister, the company toured the US and Canada. One year later, she was playing secondary roles and understudying principal ones. By 1936, she showcased those roles on another US tour that included eighteen weeks in New York. By mid-1937, she was a full-fledged principal getting good reviews for both singing and acting, especially in her hometown.

Then the whole edifice came crashing down. Another soprano began taking over her roles, and at the end of 1938, she left the company. The official line was that she left to pursue other theatrical work, and that she was really too tall for those soprano roles anyway, but the truth was that she was romantically involved with the musical director, and they needed him more than they did her. So she was asked to resign. It must have been like getting kicked out of Eden and losing her sole source of income in the process.

Drummie and Goddie (as everyone called Isidore Godfrey) must have gotten together fairly early on. There's a newspaper photo of the two of them standing next to each other, smiling and waving, among a group of D'Oyly Carte principals on the deck of the ocean liner *Carinthia*, just arrived in New York for the 1936 American tour. They stand comfortably close, his arm raised in an almost protective wave behind her. She's the taller of the two.

I'm convinced, based solely on intuition, that he fell for her the minute he heard her sing. They had by all accounts a good marriage, a partnership based as much on work as on love. They were demons for work. Achieving perfection was what drove them both, and both were matter-of-fact about it, self-effacing, even. As the company's musical director, Godfrey would have worked with her on polishing her performances, and she would have been a rewarding pupil. Clearly there was mutual attraction, but just as clearly, there was a meeting of minds.

Both, in different ways, were outsiders. Drummie was Scottish, not at all the same as being English, and Godfrey was a Jew, a son of observant Polish immigrants. He was as assimilated as a Jew could be, but in Britain, as elsewhere, a Jew was always a Jew. So both wore an invisible badge of otherness that each would have recognized.

There's no recording of Drummie in her soprano roles, and I wish there were. I'd give a month of my life—maybe more—to hear her as Princess Ida. But there is a scratchy 78 rpm disc privately recorded on tour in New York, probably in 1937, on which she announces majestically: "This is Ann Drummond-Grant. I'm going to sing 'Comin' Thro' the Rye,' accompanied by Mister Isidore Godfrey." In the ringing soprano she retained even in her contralto years, she sings four verses in Scots dialect. One might read a coded message in the text, though I'm inclined not to:

> Gin a body meet a body
> Comin' frae the well
> Gin a body kiss a body
> Need a body tell? . . .

> Mang the train there is a swain
> I dearly lo'e mysel,
> But what his name or whaur his hame
> I dinna care to tell.

As for Isidore Godfrey's marriage, to a former D'Oyly Carte chorister named Marguerite Kynaston—I want very much to say it was petering out by the time Drummie came along. Clearly, he wasn't spending much time with his wife, whom he probably met when he joined the company in 1925. She left it in 1929, so he would have been touring without her for four years when he met Drummie. Proximity and sympathy did their work.

Marguerite Kynaston had been married before, and she may have been reluctant to be divorced a second time. Whatever the reason, it wasn't until June 1940 that Goddie and Drummie were finally able to marry, in a civil ceremony. (Before the registrar, like Ko-Ko and Katisha.) According to the marriage record, both were residing at 40 Maida Vale in London. I don't know how long they lived together before marrying, but it strikes me as an extraordinary leap of faith for a woman of that time and strict religious upbringing. She may have had little choice, having no regular income and no family money. But it's clear they wanted to be together. For the next ten years of Drummie's exile from the D'Oyly Carte, they had to fight for it.

36

MASTER CLASS, 1972

BY THE END OF MY FIRST YEAR of music school, it was clear I cared for the piano more than I cared for singing, though I'd pledged my life to following in Drummie's footsteps. When I sang, I was all too aware of what I couldn't do; at the piano, I could engage directly with music at a level that satisfied. A feeling of worthiness doesn't come from achieving perfection but from the right kind of striving.

I certainly didn't feel worthy as a woman. I thought I was in love with Richard, and he wasn't having it. He responded to my heightened emotions by telling me I was too unstable to face the real world. He also told me I didn't know how to have fun, which was arguably true.

But then he and his brother did something wonderful: they sent a bunch of their students upstate for a week of master classes in Lake Placid. The organizers of the music festival were waiving tuition because they needed pianists. Which was how I, who never presumed to call myself a pianist, experienced teaching at the highest level. It shook me awake.

I'd never heard of the pianist giving the classes, György Sebök, so I wandered into the shabby, sweltering studio in the old Olympic Stadium building with no expectations. I saw, seated at one of two side-by-side grand pianos, a slight, barrel-chested man of fifty with a cigarette and an enigmatic smile. He was always, always wreathed in smoke unless he was actually playing—sometimes even then if he left the cigarette in his mouth. The smile, though not always visible, was always implied.

Sebők was Hungarian ("from Szeged, where the paprika comes from," he said), and he spoke in a soft, heavily accented baritone that dropped tantalizingly at the ends of words. Before I knew how important he was, I could see that he not only knew everything about piano playing—he seemed to have the entire repertoire in his fingers—but that he also knew about people. He approached each student differently, sensing who they were, what they were thinking, how best to reach them. He could see if a pianist was holding tension in her mouth or thinking about tiny details instead of the larger narrative of a piece. I had never encountered anyone so present, so fluent at imparting wisdom, so relaxedly in command.

He spun useful metaphors all day long. Music, he said, must happen in the mind before it happens in the body; solving technical problems requires learning new ways of thinking. His advice was deeply practical: "Playing faster is like shifting gears in a car: you make it happen by adjusting your thinking." But he was also philosophical: "Don't represent the composer's inner fight—*fight* it." Or: "Now I have the feeling that you told the story of a note, which is long; instead of that you initiated a note, which survived."

One of Fred's students had come to Lake Placid with us. When he introduced himself by saying he studied with Frederick Marvin, Sebők gave him a blank look: the name meant nothing to him. But he had strong opinions about the Arrau technique with its relaxed, rotating wrists. It sounded passive to him. "If I have to undergo surgery," he said, "I don't want a surgeon who holds the knife like *this*"—miming the exact way Fred held his hands at the keyboard.

A strong, beautiful sound, he said, can't be produced by relaxing. It requires an elegant balance of tension and release: using the arms as weighted pendulums that drop the hands on the keys and lift them again. When he worked with John Contiguglia's best student, a serious pianist who'd brought a serious Beethoven sonata, he took the harshness out of her sound by showing her how to open her arms between notes. Her playing was excellent, but he made it better.

As for little amateur me, I couldn't feel nervous or intimidated around him, only calm and engaged. It seemed perfectly natural to play for him, though I was fathoms out of my depth. I produced my Liszt piece, "Saint Francis of Assisi Preaching to the Birds." Francis does his preaching in orotund octaves. Sebök asked me, gently, "What language would he have been speaking?" Oh. Italian! I played the passage again, thinking of the caressing sounds of Italian, and suddenly it came together, in my mind and in my hands.

Sebök's own playing was gorgeous. Loud or soft, fast or slow, it had an authority, a rightness. ("The truth has a special ring," he said.) The sound was rich, the style true to the composer. He made difficult passages sound easy but never facile. When he demonstrated a piece for a student, he never needed to look at the music; he'd already mastered and retained it. Why hadn't I heard of him?

I've neglected to mention that the other big presence at this little festival was the cellist Janos Starker, whom I certainly had heard of. He and Sebök had a famous chamber music partnership and had studied together in Budapest before events (the German invasion in 1944, the Communist crackdown in 1956) made life in Hungary untenable. Now their home base was Indiana University, where they were master teachers.

We got to watch them coach chamber music ensembles that week. Starker was regally assertive, reminding us of Yul Brynner in *The King and I*, while Sebök exuded an animated, almost feline contentment. They taught with enormous joy, finishing each other's sentences and engaging in what appeared to be competitive chain-smoking. Their joy was contagious; the players blossomed.

In the evenings, they gave recitals. I turned pages for Sebök, unable to resist volunteering—I had to be in the middle of that music. I was out of my depth there, too, not being a brilliant sight reader. But I pretended I was. (He basically knew the music anyway.) After one recital, I asked Starker why Sebök wasn't more famous. He replied that he was a very great pianist but completely without ambition, entirely uninterested in fame.

This was not merely a matter of temperament. When the Germans invaded Hungary, Sebök—barely in his twenties and already a concert artist—was conscripted into forced labor with the other Jews. For two years, he broke boulders into gravel for roads. He spoke of this once in class: how his hands had been transformed into a mass of rock-hard calluses, and he'd thought he would never play again. But after a time, he said, he was able to peel the calluses off like a glove. "And then I sat down at the piano and played 'La Campanella'"—a dazzlingly difficult Liszt étude.

Sebök has been quoted as saying that his wartime experience "reduced him to zero," forcing him to rethink everything he had learned. The concept of rebuilding was central to his teaching. "After a certain age," he said, "one constantly destroys oneself and builds again." I was stirred by this idea, though at nineteen, I had no context for understanding it. It was a Zen-master sort of thing to say, and there was something of the Zen master about Sebök, though I believe he would have characterized himself as a seeker rather than a master.

As I said, he observed everyone, and that week, he saw me as I was: a half-baked student pianist who scribbled left-handedly in a notebook. A halfway decent page turner. A girl-woman, plump in places, with green eyes and long gold hair, almost pretty. Clever, but not as clever as she thought she was. Impassioned, strongly opinionated, prone to melodrama. Deeply unsure of herself and pretending the opposite. A tangle.

Yet he must have seen something he liked. On the last day of class, he paused on his way out of the studio to gently touch my hair and kiss my cheek. There, in front of everyone. No one knew why, least of all me, but I suddenly knew my own worth as a human being: a momentary awakening. I treasured that small, perfect gesture, wore it like an amulet, for years.

I wasn't the only one to feel changed by meeting Sebök, who was known far and wide as a transformative teacher. His students, rather than emerging from his studio with a specific "Sebök sound," were encouraged to grow into the musicians they were in their souls. Becoming the person you really are is a great achievement—another thing I wouldn't have understood at nineteen. I was still pursuing the path I thought I was supposed to pursue, making obeisance to a dead singer, taking direction from anyone who showed the slightest interest in me.

But a spell had been broken. The way I experienced music with Sebök and Starker made me look at my music-student life and see how grown up it wasn't. I couldn't go back to playing mind games with Richard, let alone to thinking I was in love with him. I'd ginned up a crush that wasn't real, and it wasn't doing me, or him, any good. It had to stop.

37

METHOD ACTING

THE FALL SEMESTER BEGAN. My roommate, Jeannie, and I had conned our way into a large, casement-windowed room in the French House, where everybody was supposed to speak French and nobody did. Jeannie opined that Richard had been stringing me along, but I knew that wasn't the case. It was more like what Gertrude Stein said about Oakland: there was no *there* there.

It took the Contiguglias months to pack themselves off to Europe. The night we said goodbye, after the last in a series of farewell parties, Richard gave me a ride to the French House. When we got there, he cut the motor and said, "Kiss me."

Before I could stop myself, I said, "*Why?*" Then, absurd as it felt, I kissed him on the mouth, briefly. John was in the back seat. I kissed him too.

I was glad they were leaving. I couldn't go on falling prey to the emotions they called forth. But if I had decided to study acting to please Richard and John, why on earth was I doing it now? Too late to ask. I was officially a drama student.

I still took voice lessons and wouldn't give up piano lessons. I auditioned for Fred Marvin, trotting out Saint Francis and his twittering birds one last time, amazed that I wasn't the least bit nervous. (That was Sebök's doing. I remembered how impassively he'd sat when someone was playing, his cigarette in its little gold holder. He was a voice in my head: *Don't worry. Think. Relax.*) Fred was favorably surprised and said so, and then gave me a list of pieces to learn.

I didn't have time to learn them. I'd enrolled in a senior-level poetry workshop—I wrote sonnets—and the obligatory music history courses. And German. Theater classes, in a remote part of campus, took up a large part of my day. I could no longer pound a piano for hours on end, which meant I couldn't benefit from whatever Fred was trying to impart.

Acting class was a revelation on several levels. Being a beginner, I was placed with freshmen, kids who had carted their dreams from all over the country. More than the music students, whose primary relationships were with their instruments and their teachers, the drama students yearned to relate to an audience. It was all they'd ever wanted. To me they seemed even more messed up than the music students—more vulnerable, more sensitive to criticism—something I hadn't thought possible.

I thought I could tell which of them had star quality, though what I was probably seeing was training and experience. Speaking and moving onstage are things that can be taught. Unfortunately for some of us, the SU Drama Department was committed to method acting, which meant that classic stage-craft took a back seat to emotional authenticity. We spent most of that semester in leotards, dredging up feelings.

Actually it was fun, completely different from what I was used to. Unlike the first weeks at music school, when I'd listened to my classmates in order to judge them and decide who I was better than, I was now part of a group of strangers starting from scratch. We didn't do scenes or learn lines. We stood in a large circle on a semi-dark stage, attempting to become aware of our bodies and the vocal instruments therein. All of us, instructors included, wore leotards and tights. I felt exposed, unable to hide my breasts or belly or thighs—but everyone else was just as exposed, and nobody seemed to care what they or I were shaped like. We were there to experience movement and speech in a primal way.

Our acting teacher, Maria Wida, was Hungarian, with an accent even thicker than Sebök's. I found it comforting. Hungarians, I decided, were my teachers of destiny. I remember her as tall, though I don't think she was. She said she was thirty-five but looked older. She was both lean and voluptuous, with strong, aristocratic features and a mane of curly brown hair. She moved like a dancer, and indeed she was one: she'd taught at a Fred Astaire studio when she first came to the US.

Maria was passionate about connecting with each one of us. I didn't think she liked me because I could never answer a question to suit her; I was too verbal and cerebral. Soon I stopped trying to show how smart I was and started listening and observing. My sort of smartness was useless here.

I believed acting was glorified pretending, which I was good at, but only through the medium of words. I'd never considered what it might mean to pretend with my body. Once again, in a new context, I found myself estranged from everything below the neck.

We did a lot of silent exercises. In one, we were asked to find total relaxation onstage in an overstuffed armchair lit by a single spotlight. One by one, watched by the rest of the class, we sat or slumped or sprawled in that chair, accompanied by a lugubrious orchestral recording of something by Liszt. Maria could tell who was genuinely relaxed, and I wasn't. I was too conscious of being looked at.

In another exercise, we were paired off and asked to portray, wordlessly, a swallow in love with a reed, an image drawn from a story by Oscar Wilde. ("The Happy Prince." Maria was obsessed with it.) I was the reed, kneeling, rooted in the ground and moving with the wind. My swallow, an acting instructor who sometimes attended the class, answered my movements with a sensuous dance, and I began to respond in kind. It was a very sexy little exercise. I felt embarrassed afterward and told him I was too fat to be a reed. He said, sternly, that he'd seen me as beautiful and slender: I *was* that damn plant. It may have been the most genuine performance of my acting career.

Which consisted of exactly one tiny part in one forgettable play—so forgettable I can't remember anything about it except that I was one of two nurses' aides force-feeding a comatose patient. My erstwhile swallow tried to help me imagine what it would be like to be on my feet all day doing such thankless, exacting work. I couldn't feel it, but the part was so small as to be basically actor-proof. We rehearsed and rehearsed. I spent a lot of time standing around, i.e., not writing poems or learning a Beethoven sonata or singing. The play went well, but after the run was over and I had the pleasure of tearing the sets apart, I didn't audition for anything else. I'd neglected my other classes and needed to catch up.

Maria, bless her, kept trying to figure out who I was and how to reach me. Once, after a gathering in her apartment, I tidied her kitchen, and she noticed how I wrapped a bit of lemon before putting it in the fridge. This, she said, indicated a precision and organization that could help me in my work. She herself, she said, lacked that ability, and though it made her physically sick to live in a mess, she was incapable of getting organized. I offered to help, starting with the piles of papers in her office. We didn't get far. We just talked.

She complained bitterly that she couldn't meet interesting men. She scared them off, she said, and asked if I had a boyfriend. When I told her about my crush on my unresponsive piano teacher, she laughed her loud laugh with an edge like an infant's cry. "You have the most believable absurdity about you," she said. "You have a way of making situations that would be ridiculous for anyone else seem perfectly acceptable. You should really be Gwendolen. You know Wilde's Gwendolen? If anyone should play that part, it's you."

Perhaps she did see me clearly. Gwendolen is the pert love interest in Oscar Wilde's *The Importance of Being Earnest*, a play that owes quite a lot to W.S. Gilbert. Maria had spotted the Victorian girl in her class.

I'd met Maria within a month of meeting Sebök but didn't realize that she, like him, had been "reduced to zero" during the war. She seemed a puzzling mix of strength and woundedness. Though she had enormous authority as a teacher, and we all loved her, she seemed always to be asking for our approval. She struggled to overcome the thick accent that limited the roles she could play. I remember her trying and failing to master Hamlet's lines: "Give me that man / That is not passion's slave, and I will wear him / In my heart's core, ay, in my heart of heart." I thought she belonged in some cosmopolitan place where she didn't stick out like a brilliantly plumed bird among sparrows.

I know now, having watched her 1995 testimony for the US Memorial Holocaust Museum, that Maria was, literally and metaphorically, a displaced person. She was indeed older than she admitted, by ten years. As a Jewish teenager in Budapest during the war, she'd escaped death several times. She said she had a cockroach's instinct for knowing when and where to scuttle out of danger. Those around her—including her father, murdered in Mauthausen—were not as lucky.

After the war, when the Communists confiscated everything that hadn't already been stolen by the Nazis, Maria married, then divorced, the handsome boyfriend who had saved her life. She fled the country after the failed revolution of 1956, narrowly making it across the Austrian border. She arrived in the US riddled with survivor's guilt, with no confidence, no sense of belonging, no identity as a Jew. Her life's work was not becoming an actress, as I'd thought, but clawing her way back to a sense of her own worth.

Through all those years, she said, she found strength in her physical body. The life force in her spine held her up and held her together. This was why she began every acting class by having us fill our lungs and bodies with breath, bend at the waist, and roll up, vertebra by vertebra. It was, I now realize, her affirmation of existence.

38

ESCAPE

I DIDN'T LOVE ACTING ENOUGH to pursue it with the necessary fervor, and after a semester among serious acting students, I knew it. I couldn't imagine entering a profession where constant rejection was the norm. Nor did I have the requisite talent. If my body was my instrument, I couldn't play it. I had no sense of what people saw when they looked at me; I was like a child who thinks she can make herself invisible by closing her eyes.

My eyes themselves were problematic—they tended to cross without my realizing it. I have a congenital strabismus that my father never bothered to tell me about, though it ran in his family. The condition is neurological and untreatable. I'm sure he figured that since nothing could be done about it, I was better off not knowing, but it bedeviled me from the start. I grew up unconsciously craning my neck so as not to see double. This made me look conceited, messed with my cervical spine, and—now that I think about it—accounted for my rotten coordination in gym class. It's probably also why my mother never thought I was pretty. But I was clueless until my thirties, when an ophthalmologist told me what was going on and suggested that prisms might help. (They do, somewhat.) It might have been useful to know, as an acting student, that I was physically incapable of casting a sidelong glance.

Never mind. The impetuous cross-eyed girl was hell bent on becoming an impetuous cross-eyed woman, and the SU Drama Department did me a huge favor. It got me out of town.

One fall afternoon, our lecture on the Theatre of Cruelty was interrupted by a professor seeking students for the semester abroad in Amsterdam. It was a third-year program, but enrollment was low, so they were reaching out to sophomores. Studying drama in a Dutch-speaking country made a lot less sense than studying it in London, where there was a larger, better program. But I scented the heady air of escape, and without thinking it through even a little, I said, "Sign me up!"

I applied without telling my parents. Lucille Sack thought it would be better if I presented it to them as a fait accompli. She wrote me a recommendation, part of which the administrator shared in my interview: "She says you're a lady, and that you'll eat anything." Once I was accepted, I told Mother I would be spending the next semester in Amsterdam.

"Amsterdam . . . New York?"

"Nope. Amsterdam, Holland." It wasn't going to cost much more than a semester in Syracuse, and I wasn't going to be talked out of it. My parents didn't try. I'd be living with a Dutch family, which must have seemed safer than letting me roam free on a Eurail Pass as my brothers had. Besides, my father wanted me to experience Europe. He'd gone to medical school in Innsbruck before the war—American schools had quotas for Jews back then—and he knew the importance of a fresh perspective.

Most of my friends at school were likewise leaving town. Jeannie was transferring to Barnard College in New York, where her boyfriend—she now had a real boyfriend—had gotten a job as a journalist. The better music students were scattering to better schools.

Even Lisa, though she stayed in Syracuse, left the music

school, having had enough of the miserable place. She kept up her lessons with Fred, but after a while she'd had enough of him too. She never spoke ill of him afterward. She'd already begun teaching piano lessons, and now she set about devising a schedule that would allow her to retire comfortably one day. She loved finding ways to motivate her students without bullying or belittling them, and her methods got results: she always had a long waiting list. She had adopted a strategy of militant kindness and compassion, and it worked well for her.

One night before I left for Amsterdam, I rode with Lisa as she drove through some of her favorite neighborhoods. Back in our Days of Fred, we used to do this endlessly, stopping in front of houses we especially liked. Now we knew what all the houses looked like and just kept going. As we drove down one wooded, winding suburban road, a voice began singing in my head and wouldn't be silenced: Ann Drummond-Grant. She hadn't visited me in recent months; even when I summoned her, she wouldn't come. She was like that, turning up on her own schedule, like a comet. Now I heard her as clearly as if I were hearing a recording or the voice itself. I took it as an omen.

39

THE WAR
(1940-1945)

I WAS BORN BARELY EIGHT YEARS AFTER the end of World War II, but it seemed to belong to the distant past—to that time when all the movies, even the cartoons, were black and white, and women wore strange rolled hairstyles and huge shoulder pads and sang like the Andrews Sisters. The war was over. Peace and prosperity were the norm and always would be.

I didn't realize how that war was still shaping my life and that of everyone I knew. It loomed so large I couldn't see it.

When I was a child at summer camp, the director's wife, a radiant young woman named Hedwig Rose, told us how, as a child in Amsterdam, she'd once been allowed to go for a walk without wearing the yellow star because she didn't "look" Jewish. She didn't add that most of her family had been murdered at Auschwitz, or that she had spent four years in hiding and nearly starved to death during the "hunger winter" of 1944–45, or that her mother did die, right next to her, in their tiny hiding place. We couldn't see the story Hedy carried. She later became an educator who devoted her life to telling it.

My tiny Yiddish grandmother, widowed when I was four, was withdrawn and depressed all the years I knew her. She never talked about the shtetl she left around the turn of the twentieth century. When the Nazis invaded, the Jews there were rounded up and shot—this happened all over Poland. I don't know how many family members we lost. My friend Joby's (tiny, widowed) Yiddish grandmother was just as helpless and depressed, just as superstitious and suspicious. I thought it was simply the way Yiddish grandmothers were.

My father's parents never really left the shtetl. They'd had to scramble there, and they'd scrambled in America too. They read a Yiddish newspaper and spoke an English that was decidedly broken. Their first two children, my father and his sister Dorothy, were quiet and studious, but the third child, Lillian, was exuberant and big-boned like my grandfather. During the war, she helped out at the dry-cleaning plant and drove the delivery truck; if it broke down, she opened the hood and fixed it. Exposure to the dry-cleaning chemicals may have hastened her death from tuberculosis at twenty-nine. I never met her.

It was my father's sense of duty as a first-generation American that made him enlist after Pearl Harbor, abandoning my pregnant mother, who never forgave him. It was his war experience, never talked about, that made him drill into my brothers the idea that they had to leave the world a better place, preferably by becoming doctors, something they neither wanted nor were suited for.

As for England during the war—well, I had a hazy idea of that too. I knew there were hardships, which, at a distance of decades, had been sentimentalized into situations requiring stiff upper lips. The reality was harrowing. Ann Drummond-Grant and Isidore Godfrey were married in London shortly before the Blitz, in which tens of thousands were killed and hundreds of thousands lost their homes.

When war broke out in September 1939, the Home Office announced that all theaters, cinemas, and places of entertainment would be closed. Rupert D'Oyly Carte immediately disbanded his opera company, putting everyone, including Isidore Godfrey, out of a job. When theaters reopened after just three weeks, Carte had to hustle to pull the company back together. Soon, one by one, the men of the D'Oyly Carte went off to war, leaving the company's male cohort smaller and older as retired players stepped in for the recruits.

The D'Oyly Carte continued to tour. But now there were blackouts, air raids—some during performances—and theaters reduced to rubble. The trains that carried the company from one venue to the next were crammed with soldiers. The usual "digs" (theatrical boarding houses) were occupied by families who had been bombed out of their homes. And very early on, in November 1940, the company's London warehouse was destroyed in the Blitz. Sets and costumes for four operas, including the mainstay *Pinafore*, went up in smoke.

Despite all this, the players were expected to sparkle. They had to, for the sake of their war-worn audiences. And sparkle they did, thanks in large part to their unassuming, formidably disciplined musical director. It's no exaggeration to say that Isidore Godfrey pulled those performances together out of thin air.

Consider this: *He didn't have an orchestra.* Extraordinary as it seems for an opera company that was a national institution, the D'Oyly Carte picked up freelance musicians at each venue and rehearsed them into shape. During the war, this talent pool shrank alarmingly, and Goddie had to contend with last-minute substitutes who didn't know their way around their own instruments. Or showed up drunk. Or didn't, in the case of one double-bassist, have a bow. Starting in the 1950s, he was afforded the luxury of traveling with eight or nine core players, but never a full band.

Nor was he allowed to travel with full scores, because the operas were still under copyright, and management was paranoid about safeguarding Sullivan's orchestrations. (These were kept in a bank box in London. Never mind that a maze-bright composition student could probably have worked them out by listening closely to the company's recordings.) So he conducted from a piano score with important entrances marked in red—which meant, in practice, that he conducted from memory, paying scrupulous attention to every tiny detail.

Mild mannered and puckish as he seemed, Godfrey was absolutely in charge. Before he began an overture, he would silence a buzzing audience merely by turning around and looking at them. Everyone onstage knew that if they kept their eyes on him (as he not-so-gently insisted), they'd never miss an entrance. Self-deprecating in the manner of one who knows exactly how good he is, he was driven—not to advance his career, which suited him perfectly, but to uphold a very high standard, no matter what cast of characters was onstage or in the pit.

The record of his marriage to Ann Drummond-Grant reveals something fundamentally sweet about him. He describes his late father, Manus Godfrey, as having been "of independent means." This made me think there was family money, but there was no money in that family other than what the Godfrey children brought in. Manus Godfrey, a violist, was so crippled by arthritis he couldn't work at all.

Those Godfrey children were hugely talented. Anne, born in 1888, was a concert violinist who played a command performance for the king. Freda, one year younger, embarked on a major acting career at the age of twelve, when she sailed to South Africa (in the care of a famous actor-manager named Leonard Rayne) and became a star. Her income alone was enough to support the family.

Isidore, born in 1900, was a serious pianist. I know this because he won a prize as a conservatory student for his interpretation of the last movement of Beethoven's *Hammerklavier* sonata—the biggest, thorniest, craziest fugue ever written for piano, certainly not a student piece and arguably not play-able by anyone. When he was offered the position of assistant conductor and chorus master at the D'Oyly Carte at age twenty-four, he jumped at it. Not only was it what he wanted, it was a steady job. As I've said, he was a child of immigrants.

His parents were observant Jews who had come to London from a city near Warsaw in the Pale of Settlement—in Poland but controlled by Russia. Goddie's birth name was Israel Gotfryd; he became Isidore Godfrey when the family was nat-uralized in 1905. When I found the naturalization certificate online, I stared and stared at it. Manus Gotfryd was born in the District of Plotzk in a town transliterated as "Tchachanoff." Today this would be written as the town of Ciechanow in the district of Plock. It's the town my father's family came from, where all the Jews were shot. Goddie's parents and my grand-parents had walked the same streets, eaten the same bread, and made the same decision to get the hell out.

Well . . . perhaps. I used to think the Jews in the Pale of Settlement were all impoverished like Tevye the dairyman in *Fiddler on the Roof*, and that they had to leave their wretched shtetls to avoid being killed in the pogroms. There's truth to this. When Russia annexed Poland, it was indeed open season on Jews, and that was fine with a lot of the Poles. But some Jews in cities like Ciechanow led middle-class lives, ran busi-nesses, and traveled freely. They knew it wouldn't be easy to uproot themselves but did so for all kinds of reasons.

My father's father, one of seven children whose father tended cattle for a living, accompanied his brother's pregnant wife to America (in steerage, with water sloshing in the bot-tom of the boat) so she could join her husband in Syracuse. A cousin of mine left for America to avoid being conscripted in the Russo–Japanese War. Another was sent there by his parents, who worried that his Polish friends would talk him into becoming Catholic. (They sold a cow to pay for his passage, as Tevye might have done.) My father's mother was orphaned and forced to work as a maid in a wealthy household—or so said her cousin Fanny, many years later. She left so she'd never again have to be anyone's servant.

Isidore Godfrey's parents would seem to have come from a more cultured stratum of shtetl society, but they, too, made the calculation that their lives as Jews would be better abroad— even though there were anti-Semites everywhere. It didn't matter who you were or where you settled: if you were a Jew, you wore the yellow star, metaphorically if not physically. You knew this even if you were the impeccably British musical director of a beloved British opera company.

40

PRINCIPAL BOY

AND DRUMMIE? I DON'T THINK SHE TOURED with her husband while he slogged around the country putting on the operas and God knows how many concerts for the troops. Like most British women, she was part of the war effort, joining the ATS (Auxiliary Territorial Service), the women's branch of the army. There's a photograph of her looking very trim in uniform, serving tea and sandwiches to the cast at an open-air performance of The Gondoliers in London in 1943. I suspect much of her military service was of the tea-and-sandwiches variety, sandwiched between theatrical engagements of her own. An entertainer's greatest contribution, after all, is to entertain.

This was the decade when Drummie gained the experience that her D'Oyly Carte colleagues spoke of so admiringly. She learned her way around a stage—how to move, how to stand, how to make the most of her lines, how to deal with other people's flubs. She became an expert makeup artist. As principal contralto in the fifties, she was generous with this knowledge, taking younger players under her wing and coaching them in ways they found invaluable.

I haven't been able to find much of a record of her work in the forties, but there seems to have been plenty of it. She says so herself, in that radio interview she and Goddie did in San Francisco during the 1955 American tour. It's the only recording I have of her everyday speaking voice: thoughtful, low, mellifluous, with a trace of a Scottish burr. Her laugh, which her colleague Cynthia Morey described as "mournful," is exactly that: slow and doleful, like dark water lapping the side of a boat. She speaks quietly, with a resonance that conveys tremendous authority.

Asked how she was able to sing both soprano and contralto roles, Drummie says it's not unusual for a voice to deepen with the years, "especially a dramatic soprano voice, which covers a very big range." She says this matter-of-factly, though a voice like hers is rare and hard to handle, requiring enormous care as it matures. She makes it clear—even in this little radio interview—that she expects nothing less than perfection of herself, and that she relishes the work it takes. Her talk is so lilting and easy to listen to that you almost don't notice there's no frivolity in it; she's all discipline, and the discipline runs deep.

After leaving the company in 1938, she says, she did "straight work, revue, musical comedy, and pantomime"—explaining for American listeners that these are children's entertainments put on at Christmastime. "I did *seven* Christmas seasons of pantomime as a principal boy," she says, "in tights, and dashing around." She laughs as she says this. Principal boys, the heroes of these fairytale extravaganzas, were played by shapely young women in form-fitting costumes. At the time of her interview, Drummie was just shy of fifty and had acquired a bit of contralto-appropriate heft. She favored tweed suits, button-down blouses, and ladylike hats. It would have been hard to imagine her dashing around in tights. But I have visual evidence that she wore them extremely well.

This, once again, is thanks to Cynthia Morey, to whom Drummie presented a photo of herself in full panto regalia as Dick Whittington, tall and elegant in a tunic, tights, high heels, and Peter Pan cap. Her legs, not visible in any of her

D'Oyly Carte costumes, really do seem to go on forever. She looks perfectly delighted, like your favorite Sunday school teacher showing how it's possible to be wholesome and sexy at the same time.

Drummie meant what she said about dashing around. According to Morey, who did several seasons of it, pantomime is hard work. She writes (in A *Set of Curious Chances*, the sequel to her D'Oyly Carte memoir): "Over the Christmas and New Year period, we were doing thirteen shows a week—twice nightly, plus a matinee on Saturdays. It was quite daunting to hear the stage manager in the wings saying, 'Quarter of an hour, please' as you were taking your curtain call for the previous performance." Each show was a marathon of singing, dancing, slapstick comedy, and audience participation, with multiple costume changes. You had to be bright, fresh, and energized, no matter what.

Through luck or doggedness or Drummie casting a bread-crumb trail from beyond the grave, I have actually seen her as a principal boy—fleetingly, blurrily, in black and white—in an amateur film shot in Glasgow in 1943. (It's in the Moving Image Archive of the National Library of Scotland, which cheerfully sold me a DVD.) For six silent minutes, there are quick shots of about a zillion dance numbers—sparkling girls in sparkling cos-tumes—bits of fairytale, a glimpse of the pantomime dame, and a sketch with a gyrating conductor (who I *think* is the Scottish entertainer Harry Gordon) leading a chorus into mayhem. In one of the fairytale bits, the principal boy strides onstage in a form-fitting outfit, raising her arms and commanding the stage. She's gone in seconds but reappears in a sleek evening gown for the conductor sketch, tall and regal as the lady with the torch in the Columbia Pictures logo. The production is spectacular. Nobody looks tired, but they all must be.

After the pantomime, there are two and a half minutes of

a Christmas party where cast members parade past the camera multiple times bearing food and drink. They're enjoying themselves mightily, but Drummie is not among them. During the 1943 Christmas season, the D'Oyly Carte was touring in Southport and Bolton, two hundred miles from Glasgow. Did she and Goddie find a way to be together? Most likely not, given the number of shows both were doing. She might have hopped a train to Edinburgh to spend Christmas with her sister, though she'd have had to return immediately for the shows on Boxing Day. Perhaps Agnes, who now had a three-year-old daughter, came to Glasgow to see Drummie. Or perhaps Drummie just went to her digs and slept.

There's one Christmas in the forties when I know she and Goddie were together: in 1947, when the D'Oyly Carte sailed on the *Queen Mary* for five months in New York and Boston. Some of the spouses came with them. *The Tatler* ran photos of the farewell party at the Savoy, and there, at one of the tables, sits Drummie, impeccably dressed for travel (tweed jacket, dark silk blouse, little veiled hat) and smiling radiantly at the camera. Next to her, likewise impeccably attired (three-piece suit, foulard tie, little round tortoiseshell glasses) is Goddie, distracted by a hundred details, not quite managing to smile.

41

AMSTERDAM, 1973

ONLY AS I BOARDED THE PLANE to Amsterdam in January 1973 did I realize what I'd committed myself to with barely a thought. Other than summer camp, I'd never been away from home. Stumbling through the jetway felt like falling down a chute to perdition. It didn't help that I was terrified of flying. (Even now, when I've long since gotten over it, I have an unvarying ritual of looking out the plane's window to find a capital letter A, as in Ann, somewhere in view. Once I see one, I'll look for a D or a G.)

The plane was enormous. I took my seat somewhere along the endless aisle like a Lego block being clicked into place. Next to me was a drama student I'd never met—I didn't know any of these people—a delicate blonde with watery eyes. She'd been in a play that closed the night before. "I slept with the director," she said absently. "I smell like sex." I didn't know what sex smelled like and couldn't smell anything in any case. I wondered if this was an augury for the semester, but it wasn't. I flew to Amsterdam a virgin, and a virgin I returned.

It was my first overnight flight, and I wasn't prepared for how it felt to encounter a gray February dawn in the middle of the night. Wretched and bedraggled, we were bused sixty miles to a town called Vught for a three-day orientation. I don't believe they mentioned that Vught had been the site of a concentration camp, but they might have said anything and I'd have missed it. I already had a huge cold.

We were at some sort of retreat center, a castle-like brick building in the middle of a wood. Grand and shadowy, with tall casement windows looking out on huge moss-covered trees enveloped in mist—my first taste of the bone-deep northern damp. Mostly we were there to learn rudimentary Dutch from a slender, slouching, long-haired American named Mark. "*Ik heet* Mark," he said, pronouncing "heet" as "hate." "*Hoe heet jij?*" My name's Mark; what's yours? We figured it out. I liked trying to master the broad, ungainly diphthongs, the likes of which I'd never held in my mouth, and the guttural consonants, especially the soft *g*. "Van Gogh" was pronounced something like "*fn choch.*"

"*Kijk,*" Mark would repeat when making a point. I wondered: is he calling us *kikes*? Anything was possible. But kijk, pronounced somewhere between kike and cake, turned out to mean "look." I saw that Dutch was similar to German but easier, without the pesky cases. Dutch nouns, like German ones, were gendered, but masculine and feminine nouns took the same definite article, *de*, while neuter nouns took *het*. If you couldn't remember a noun's gender, you could neuter it by adding the diminutive suffix *je*. This was something I could focus on.

We were bused to Amsterdam and deposited with our families. I was to stay at the home of a Lutheran pastor in the Rooseveltlaan, a broad busy avenue of formidably neat redbrick apartment buildings with lace-curtained bay windows framed in white—about as Dutch as Dutch could be. The apartment was on the second floor, which was actually the third floor because in Europe the first floor was called the ground floor, *begane grond* in Dutch. *Bechhana chhront.* I would be muttering gutturally to myself the entire time I was in Holland.

My room was tiny, maybe twelve feet long by eight feet wide, with one large window looking out on the busy avenue. A desk—no drawers, just a writing surface—had been installed under the window. Space was so tight that the end of the single bed had to go under the desk, next to the chair. I was dismayed by this setup when I arrived with my huge red suitcase but noted with pleasure the little vase of flowers on the desk. Not quite flowers. Buds, which turned out to be daffodils. In February! I soon learned that even in the dead of winter, flowers (preferably buds—*knopjes*) were presented at every opportunity.

The girl I'd sat next to on the plane was shocked when I told her about my room. She wondered how I'd ever be able to take a lover, especially in the home of a pastor. As though I could be so cavalier about sex. The truth was that I didn't know who I was or what I was doing in Amsterdam. So I dissolved into the place to see who I would become. The Roodenburg family would be mine, and I would live by its rules and rituals. It was the only workable option, since every activity in that household was exquisitely choreographed, measured by the ticking and striking of multiple antique clocks. (One was tall and stood in a corner. Another was French and tolled the hour twice.) They had boarded six students before me—for the income, I supposed—so it was for me, not them, to learn the drill.

42

MOEDER
AND VADER

THE ROODENBURGS, WHOM I WAS encouraged to call *Moeder* and *Vader*, were in their early fifties. They had raised three tall sons, one of whom, Jan, still lived in a flat upstairs. Moeder was tiny and round-faced and spoke beautiful Dutch in a high fluty voice. She was endlessly industrious, shopping and cooking and keeping the place so immaculate it seemed to clean itself. When she noticed a run in one of my turtlenecks, she darned it—I'd never known anyone who darned. Yet she was capable of great stillness. There was no quiet like the quiet of afternoon tea in that home. On her writing desk was a framed handwritten motto, *Éternel, je me confie en toi.*

Vader, the pastor, was tall and gentle, with soft, soft hands. His head hung forward in the manner of one who buries himself in books, to the point where he had become almost humpbacked. He had a long face with a cleft chin and little blue eyes; his smile was slow, shy, and utterly genuine. He loved reading about castles and genealogy; his own name, Pieter Cornelis Roodenburg, went back at least four hundred years. When he read through Haydn or Mozart at the upright piano, he played just as he spoke: first haltingly, then with emphasis.

Vader had studied Latin, Greek, and Hebrew and was fluent

in English, German, and French. But his wife (he always referred to her as "my wife") told me that when they first married, she had to keep telling him that people would be interested in what he had to say, that no one would think him stupid.

What he was, was reverent. I knew the real thing when I saw it. Every other Sunday, he presided over services at a seventeenth-century Lutheran church in the Spui, a street in the oldest part of the city. (He traveled to other parishes on alternate Sundays.) I attended several times out of a mix of curiosity and family feeling. I remember the place as magnificent but somehow meager. And chilly. Lutheranism seemed to involve willful deprivation. I looked down from the balcony as the not-large congregation stumbled through Martin Luther's unadorned chorales, almost drowned out by the huge organ. (Where was Bach? It was as though he'd never been born. He was Lutheran too, wasn't he?) But Vader was transfigured, standing in his long black robe at a table where two white candles in great brass candlesticks flickered fiercely. He radiated the solace he found in the love of *Onze Heer Jesus Christus*.

I could only experience this solace at a clinical distance. The one big thing I'd been taught about Jesus was that we Jews didn't believe in him. I'd had a friend in high school, a fellow soprano, who felt genuinely sad that I'd be consigned to hell because I hadn't accepted Jesus as my Lord and Savior. But we Jews didn't believe in hell either, or in the notion that anyone had died to save us. There was abundant recent evidence that we were not to be saved in any sense of the word, even if we converted.

Vader didn't proselytize. He didn't have to. His faith spoke for itself. There was one Sunday when he baptized ten small children from Suriname, which was still a Dutch colony. They and their mothers were dark-skinned and dressed in their bright best, in contrast with the doughy, drably attired

Hollanders. The mothers carried lush bouquets of tulips and carnations. The children, fidgeting happily, clutched rhythm instruments, waiting to sing their carefully rehearsed hymns. What impressed me most was Vader's tender smile as he blessed each child and anointed its forehead three times, in the name of *de Vader, de Zoon, en de Heilige Geest.* He seemed to wish great things for them all. This, I thought, was what it meant to be a man of God.

I attended exactly one Friday night service at the liberal synagogue around the corner from the Roodenburgs, thinking I might find a home there. It was a new building that might have stood anywhere in the US. The congregation was small, but everyone could read Hebrew, which wasn't the case at the synagogue I grew up in. The service was in Dutch, and I couldn't follow it. Afterward, at the Oneg Shabbat (where people had to pay for their beverages, also not the case at my temple), I introduced myself to the rabbi, who—unlike the open-hearted Lutherans—didn't seem particularly interested in welcoming me to the community. In a corner, without frame or comment, hung an enlarged photo of Anne Frank.

I later visited the Anne Frank house. She was still there.

43

THE SINGING
TEACHER

OUR CLASSES WERE HELD IN A HOUSE in the Jacob Obrecht-straat, near the museums and the great concert hall, the Concertgebouw. I'm sure I took some sort of theater class, but I'm damned if I can remember it. We didn't go to plays because they were all in Dutch. The drama department was planning a class trip to London, which required a frantic getting of money from home—frantic in slow motion, since it took my letters at least eight days to get to Syracuse. But theater was not the main event; Amsterdam was. Its history could be seen and felt all around us, in the centuries-old buildings and canals, the streets named for Dutch artists and composers, the lovingly maintained infrastructure. The city's coat of arms, a red shield with three white St. Andrew's crosses on a black band, was emblazoned with pride on buildings, lamp posts, manhole covers, even garbage trucks. Syracuse had no such pride.

Young art historians who spoke perfect English walked us through the Rijksmuseum to show us the works of the great seventeenth-century Dutch painters. There were the prosperous merchants and their wives, dressed in black silk with white ruffled collars that spoke of money, their plain, open faces identical to those in Vader's congregation. There, too, were the landscapes with vast watery skies I could see in real life simply by looking up. (Amsterdam is below sea level; the sky really does look like that.) Walking the streets and canals of the city, I saw what the painters saw. This did something to my sense of time: it was clear that past and present were not distant from each other, but side by side.

When I visited the Rijksmuseum a few years ago, it was so jammed with tourists I could hardly see the paintings. In 1973, we could walk right up to them, step back, then walk up again. I learned to love Rembrandt by being in the same room with him. Ditto Van Gogh, who didn't yet have a museum of his own. His brushstrokes were physical blows to my eyes. (*Kijk. Kijk.*)

I needed a voice teacher. The university was looking into it. I wouldn't have known how to find one on my own, being too passive even to think of asking around. Mevrouw Roodenburg stepped, unbidden, into the breach. She phoned a teacher she knew of and asked what she charged for singing lessons. Of course the teacher wanted to hear me, and of course I went. Just to meet her. And out of respect for Moeder.

The signs were not good. The teacher, Anke Attema, was a large, hearty woman whose English was nonexistent. She also gave piano lessons; the student I heard as I came in was not advanced. She taught beginners, then. She seemed to know what she was doing as a singer—her speaking voice was plush, anyway. She handed me a CV with reviews and credentials, but it was in Dutch. I might have felt encouraged to know she'd been a student of the beloved Dutch soprano Jo Vincent, who, like Helen Boatwright, was known for her work in lieder and oratorio. But I hadn't heard of Jo Vincent.

Having to sing put me on the defensive. I protested that I was getting over a bad cold, that the university would have to approve a teacher of my choosing, and that I really was just coming to meet her. But Mevrouw Attema had resolute faith in herself. She assumed that because I'd shown up, I wanted to study with her. Her massive self-confidence steamrollered what little was left of my own.

Except for a few minutes of scales that afternoon, I hadn't sung at all since my last performance at a student convocation in Crouse, which had been a disaster. My semester in the drama department had gotten me out of the habit of singing for an audience; I shook uncontrollably. People told me I didn't look nervous, but I knew my voice was a light sweet ghost. So when I sang for Mevrouw Attema, I forced a bit. I don't remember what I sang, but I remember exactly how wretched it felt. If I'd added up all the moments when I took real pleasure in singing over those years, they wouldn't have amounted to a lunch break.

The voice, she said, gesticulating wildly to make up for her lack of English, was very good, but I sang with too much breath. (She meant it was breathy.) I was breathing wrong, she said, but *she* could bring out the voice, which was basically very fine. Those words were magic. I decided I liked her. But she also said she'd give me "the latest exercises," and I knew very well that vocal training was not a matter of fashion.

Then there was the contract: twenty lessons for 250 guilders. (The exchange rate was just under three guilders to the dollar.) This was extremely reasonable, especially since the university would pay half. But was it too reasonable? What was the going rate over here? Wouldn't a better teacher be more expensive? I was given twenty-four hours to decide. And I said yes—because Mevrouw Roodenburg seemed to want it, and because it was so much easier than saying no.

I don't remember what the "latest exercises" were. No, I remember one: singing *Weine Meine Reine Ein* on a descending scale, feeling the usual humiliation at the register breaks. When

THAT VOICE

Mevrouw Attema did the voice teacher thing and placed my hand on her abdomen to demonstrate breath support, I felt the usual mysterious wall of flesh. I practiced her exercises, feeling just as uncomfortable singing in the apartment with Moeder as I had singing at home with Mother. The voice refused to improve. A couple of my classmates had found a teacher they liked, but I'd signed a contract with this one. I was stuck.

44

THE CONCERTGEBOUW

THE RITUALS OF THE ROODENBURG HOME began to seem refined to the point of confinement. I was always drying dishes and putting them away, folding the tablecloth and undercloth and putting them away, bringing the tea, taking away the empty cups, setting the dinner table with each person's special fork, spoon, and napkin ring, the salt cellars, the crystal knife rests, the silver fruit knives. For breakfast and lunch, the smaller forks and knives, the jar of *suikerstroop* (thick sugar syrup), jam, chocolate sprinkles, cheese, the smaller napkin rings, the butter dish with the metal cow on the top, the long silver jam spoons.

The rituals were more satisfying than the food. My mother, a butcher's daughter, always made meat the main event: steaks, slabs of prime rib, lamb chops. Mevrouw Roodenburg would feed four adults (herself, Vader, Jan, and me) with 250 grams of beef sliced translucently thin, accompanied by heaping bowls of peeled, boiled potatoes (beloved by Jan) and chopped boiled greens, *aardappelen en groenten*. Dessert was usually fruit. My parents and I could polish off a Sara Lee Cream Cheesecake at one sitting.

I liked breakfast better because everything was eaten on slices of buttered bread, and I mean everything, including herring and chocolate. The bread was fresh, bought daily from the baker around the corner. Even the plainest Dutch cheeses were better than any I'd tasted. I ate quite a lot at breakfast. And I soon discovered there were pastry shops in every street, the better to treat myself on the way home from school. There was something called a *gember gebakje* that involved candied stem ginger and frangipane in a pastry shell. My clothes grew tighter.

For many weeks, I got no response to the chattery letters I'd dispatched to friends and family. If they were so anxious to hear from me, why the hell didn't they write? I began to feel there was something wrong with me. My eyes wouldn't focus; I couldn't concentrate in class. If someone touched me, I jumped. Somewhere inside me was a wire pulled tight; every other part of me was limp. I became hyperaware of my sloppy womanly body with its jiggly flesh.

I worried that the Roodenburgs would think me large and coarse. I shed long blonde hairs like an afghan hound, clogging the drains and snarling the vacuum cleaner. I was too disheveled and plain; no, ugly and long nosed, the Jew among the Lutherans. Clunky shoes, shapeless sweaters, tattered jeans. I walked the streets cursing the rain, the wind, and the Dutch language. There wasn't much snow in an Amsterdam winter, but there was plenty of darkness and damp.

My classmates, who were not staying with churchy folk, seemed to have an easier time adjusting. They did not try to assimilate. They went out for beers and cheap Indonesian food and availed themselves of the plentiful, not-exactly-illegal hashish that could be smoked in a rolled-up tram ticket. They talked about how weird their Dutch families were and how drunk they got on their weekend jaunts to Florence or Milan. I could only observe like an anthropologist. I was bad at drinking for sure; three sips of anything got me buzzed. (This is still the case.)

The girl from the plane invited me for drinks at the Bowl-ingcentrum, where there was a large noisy bar. She was still convinced I needed a lover, any lover. She expected her dates to end in sex: it was lovely, she said, to experience every kind of nakedness with someone you'd just met. "You can really talk to a boy after you've made love," she said. "Once you've gone to bed, you're friends for life." She sounded so casual, so free, so happy. She was also petite and pretty. I felt sure that made things easier.

It was like hearing about the joys of Jesus from the scruffy young American panhandlers in the Damrak: I could listen, but I couldn't be converted. Mevrouw Roodenburg, of course, thought that girls who hopped from bed to bed were "using themselves up." I couldn't claim any sort of moral superiority for holding onto my virginity. I was merely terrified. The hand-writing in my notebook got smaller and tighter.

Only when I was on my own—exploring the streets of Amsterdam (when it wasn't pouring), or visiting a museum, or hearing a concert—did I begin to feel like myself. Concerts were cheap, and I got student tickets for half price, so I gorged myself on music. The Concertgebouw (literally "concert build-ing") became my refuge and my shrine, as welcoming as the synagogue was not, as holy as the church was not. I went by myself, taking two trams from the Roodenburgs' flat. It didn't occur to me to ask anyone to come with me.

The first concert I heard, for under a dollar, was in the small hall, the Kleine Zaal: a piano recital by the twenty-six-year-old Murray Perahia. He looked like he hadn't the strength to shake your hand, but his playing was masterful. The hall itself was a jewel box of white marble and red velvet; the piano was a German Steinway.

The next afternoon I found myself in the Grote Zaal, which was like the small hall grown to magnificent adulthood:

the same white marble incised with the names of great composers, with a balcony surmounted by lunette windows and a
vast coffered ceiling. Smack in the middle of the stage was an
enormous pipe organ in an ornate wooden case. At the time, it
was too decrepit to be played—it's since been restored—but it
had been left in place so as not to disturb the acoustics. I was
pleased to note how the dull, scuffed wood floor contrasted
with the elegance of the place. I thought it looked like the
floor of a concert hall *should* look: used.

I had never—have never—heard anything to match
the sound in that hall: silvery, immediate, alive. New York's
Carnegie Hall, built around the same time and larger by a
thousand seats, is almost as good, but it doesn't glorify sound
the way the Concertgebouw does.

I'd come to hear Elly Ameling, the Dutch lyric soprano
who gave me hope that my own lyric voice might someday
be enough. She sang Ravel's *Shéhérazade* with the Amsterdam Philharmonic, the excellent orchestra founded by a
rosy-cheeked conductor named Anton Kersjes (*kersjes* means
"cherries"). Ameling's voice was not large or showy but clear
and pure. It carried; it shimmered in air. Standing with what I
can only describe as a radiant stillness, she sang with the kind
of ease and simplicity that's actually the product of enormous
work. She had, I thought, a wholesome glamour.

I went backstage to tell her she was my favorite soprano.
She was incredibly open and kind. "You know," she said, "some
days I think it hasn't gone so well, and I'm unhappy with my
performance, and then someone like you comes back and says
they loved it. One compares performances with other performances, but the final comparison is how much I have done
justice to the composer. To Schubert, I have only done *this*
much"—holding up her small hand with the thumb and forefinger close together. (Her Schubert was sublime.)

I didn't say how hopeless my own singing was. I told her I was studying with Anke Attema and that she seemed to be doing me good. Ameling had heard of her but knew little about her. She said it would take at least four months before I could tell if I was actually improving. By which time the semester would be over.

45

1 SAVOY HILL

ANKE ATTEMA, DAMN IT ALL, was getting too many things wrong. She assigned me a Mozart duet, "Bei Männern, welche Liebe fühlen," for her student recital, but the sheet music she gave me had been transposed to a lower key to suit the baritone I'd be singing with. I knew this would lie in the part of my voice with the worst register breaks, but she said not to worry, it wouldn't be a problem. It was. At the recital, in which all fifty-three of her dreadful students performed, the baritone was indisposed. I sang the duet with a hooty contralto who conducted herself with her elbows. We stank.

Mevrouw Attema's efforts to teach me proper support had hit a linguistic brick wall. One day she said in utter frustration, "*Je moet . . . meer toon!*" I needed more tone. Right. And how was I supposed to produce it? "*Je moet . . . persen!* Squeeze! Like you are on the toilet!" I have never forgotten this. Squeezing like you are on the toilet makes the vocal folds snap shut so no air can pass through them. She meant a different sort of squeezing but couldn't explain it. That was the moment I realized the enormity of my mistake.

It provoked the usual reaction: humiliation, followed by panic, followed by a retreat into magic realism. Ann Drummond-Grant was surely watching over me, just as she always had. If I was truly on the path to becoming a singer, someone or something would come along to light the way, and I would follow. This starts to explain why I let myself be railroaded by Mevrouw Roodenburg, who didn't know the first thing about singing or about me. I'd immediately seen that Mevrouw Attema was the wrong teacher but couldn't grant myself the agency to say so. Agency was something I didn't know I had.

At some point in the midst of all this, I went on that class trip to London. A scary little flight on a scary little plane. Surely we were there to see something wonderful, but all I remember is a lead balloon of a musical called *The Good Old Bad Old Days*. I must have skipped out on whatever else the class saw, because the D'Oyly Carte was in town, and I had to see *Iolanthe*. Isidore Godfrey wasn't in the pit; he'd retired five years before. But some of my old favorites were in the cast, and the players who were new to me were as comfortable in their roles as every player before them had been. Aside from a few barely noticeable changes, the opera was as it had always been. The D'Oyly Carte purveyed the comfort of continuity. It's the kind of comfort that can turn on you.

I didn't go backstage. Earlier that day, I'd made a pilgrimage to the D'Oyly Carte offices in the Savoy Hotel (at 1 Savoy Hill, which isn't a hill), not expecting anyone to be there on a Saturday. Someone had been: Albert A. Truelove, personal secretary to Bridget D'Oyly Carte. He remembered who I was and, with what seemed genuine interest, asked how I was doing. Sitting by his desk in a carpeted office that must have been dead quiet even on weekdays, I tried to put a bright face on things. It was hard. Two years earlier, I'd thought of myself as a singer, present tense. Now it seemed I would never learn to sing. I couldn't admit that.

It wasn't possible to see much of London in the few days I was there. I had no money and no guide, and the weather was grim. I wandered the Underground with Drummie's voice in my head, in a snippet from *Iolanthe*:

When tempests wreck thy bark,
And all is drear and dark,
If thou shouldst need an ark,
I'll give thee one.

Those lines set up a boisterously comic scene, but when Drummie sings, "drear and dark," the darkness is deep.

46

MEVROUW CITROEN

It was at the Concertgebouw that I met the next voice teacher, in the random, "preordained" way I preferred. The soloist was the twenty-seven-year-old Itzhak Perlman, who was jaw-droppingly good, the life and soul of music. I hadn't seen him before and was surprised at the aluminum crutches he used to swing himself onstage.

An elderly lady sat behind me. I'd heard her speak beautiful English to an American couple, and at intermission, I turned around. She smiled. She seemed to know Perlman, so I asked about the canes: Did he have polio?

"Yes, when he was very young," she said, and went on to tell me how she'd first heard him play the Brahms violin concerto. "I had heard it—oh, hundreds and hundreds of times—but this time, it was all new." She said she'd spent much of her life in this hall and loved it dearly. Not only did she know Perlman, she was having him to dinner along with the couple she was sitting with, a violinist and a pianist. She herself was a singer, past tense.

This was enough to loose a confessional torrent. I told her how I felt about music and how I had no faith in my voice; I told her about Herr Reutter, about Susan, about Sebök. I had no one else to talk to about these things. She said it didn't matter if your voice was small if you worked at it slowly, gradually, gently.

Finally I said, "I wish you could hear me." She handed me her card, which said, "Mevrouw Elisabeth Citroen."

I called the next day and was invited for tea. Her flat, near the Concertgebouw, was small but gave the impression of spaciousness. I expected the sitting room to be dominated by a piano but saw none; it was housed in a cabinet against one wall. The bedroom was a bohemian mélange of hats, perfumes, and a mysteriously present dress form.

Over excellent tea, served with a marvelous turnover "made of air and apples," we sounded each other out. Her enthusiasm for artistry writ small and large—perfection in pastry, the line of a piece of china, the virtuosity of a Perlman—reminded me of Lucille Sack. So did her decisiveness and brutal honesty. She was older than Lucille by I couldn't have said how much—I thought her at least sixty-five. She was actually seventy-three and Jewish, a survivor of the Nazi occupation that wiped out 75 percent of Dutch Jews. She didn't talk about that. She spoke instead of her vocal training in Berlin with one of the singers whose portraits were reverently hung in the Concertgebouw, referring to her as "my mistress," which startled me a bit. Her speaking voice was vibrant and deep, but she could no longer really sing at all. This might have been a red flag: plenty of well-trained singers have some voice left in their seventies. But not all of them.

I sang for Mevrouw Citroen, cursing inwardly that I should mutilate Schubert in this way. She said, breaking into German for some reason: "So. *Das ist der Anfang.*" That's the beginning.

She said I had to learn where to put the voice before I could do anything else and showed me a gentle humming exercise. "You must start from the beginning, the very beginning. Just this exercise first, no more," she said. "*Very* gently, like a flautist. Keep the breath *here*. No, no—make a *kiss*. Good!" She was alight, excited, lapsing into German and correcting herself, prepositions tumbling over one another. She showed me how I must make my mouth house the sound "like a church"—but not yet.

"Your singing will change," she said. "You will find it all *completely* different once you know where to put the sound." I was taken as much by her enthusiasm as by the beautiful picture she painted. I felt—yet again—the intoxicating hope that I might really learn to sing. Her method, she said, expressed years of experience in a succinct and organized manner. She deplored teachers like Attema who couldn't communicate with their students.

"Now," she said, "what shall we do?" By which she meant she wanted to teach me. Here I must confess that I actually got down on my knees next to her at the little piano. I was aware of the melodrama of the gesture, and knew it was possible I was making another mistake. But I wanted to cling to my faith in serendipity just a bit longer. And she liked me. She admired my persistence. She could see I had a "strong chin." No one else has ever said that about me. It was, however, true of Mevrouw Citroen.

We had to decide what to do about Anke Attema. I didn't care if I never saw her again, but I still had eleven lessons coming. And I didn't want to hurt her. (I don't think she'd have been hurt. She'd been paid.) We agreed I'd finish out Mevr. Attema's contract while beginning with Mevr. Citroen. I wouldn't be the only voice student to engage a second teacher on the side. But this usually happens with conservatory students who need to earn a degree but aren't satisfied with the teachers on the faculty. I would be juggling two teachers I'd chosen myself.

I said, shyly, that we needed to come to a financial arrangement. In a tone of voice that suggested it was of minimal importance, Mevrouw Citroen said she'd have to think about what to charge. "It's been so long since I've had a student. . . ."

47

WHITE RABBIT

The next day, Mevrouw Citroen called to say that her fee was seventy-five guilders per lesson—six times Anke Attema's rate. I was shocked. It was what Miss Pinnell charged, and Miss Pinnell was a full professor of singing. The Roodenburgs were scandalized. Lessons didn't cost that much in the Netherlands, they said; she was clearly after my money. I brushed them aside. What did these churchy people know? (They knew plenty, having been desperately poor and hungry during the war.)

It was hard to calculate the equivalencies. Anke Attema taught kids, not professionals. Mevrouw Citroen had studied at the highest level, or said she had. She knew Itzhak Perlman, or said she did. I was in love with the circumstance and desperate to believe her. She must have had good reason to value herself so highly.

The thing was, I had no money. What passed for my allowance was nowhere near enough. Much of it went for concerts at the Concertgebouw, where I bought the cheapest seats. I avoided restaurants but couldn't resist spending a few guilders on a pastry after school; there were days when I rode the tram home in abject terror that a controller would come along and find me without a ticket. Once I broke a dish, and Mevrouw Roodenburg asked me to pay for it. This tore a gaping hole in my budget. I'd never had to manage money before and was

mortified that I was so bad at it. Not that I ever asked my classmates what their allowances were.

Lucille Sack used to say that most of life is deciding what's
really important and acting accordingly. I wanted those lessons with Mevrouw Citroen and figured I'd manage somehow.
I must have expected the money to appear by magic, just as the
teacher had. Little came of it. We never got past the humming.
She gave me a specific sequence of soft sounds to help me place
the voice: *mee may meh mah mawh moh moo mü*. Not singing
but a prelude to singing. That was about it. I remember feeling
I wasn't getting it right.

I'll say two things in defense of Mevrouw Citroen, who I
don't believe was an out-and-out charlatan. The first is that
when she was a young student of singing—around 1920, I'd
guess—she would have had several lessons a week and been
brought along slowly and carefully by her teacher. She would
have mastered vocal technique incrementally, much as a young
ballet student has to master basic moves before learning a choreographed dance. That was how it was done in Europe in
those days. It did not apply to my life at all.

The second thing is that vocal placement really is important, just as important as breath support. It's the way the sound
resonates in the throat, mouth, and sinuses that gives a voice its
color, timbre and carrying power. A singer has to learn where
to put each note in her range to create the kind of sound she's
after. Mevrouw Citroen was right about that.

And a third thing, which I can say in hindsight: What
the hell did I expect? I was in Holland for a grand total of six
months. As Elly Ameling said, it would have taken almost that
long to see any real improvement. But I believed in magic.

Dutifully, doggedly, I kept up the lessons with both teachers,
not learning much from either. All my money went to Mevrouw Citroen. It wasn't just my pockets that were empty; *I was*

empty. I had no hope of a singing or acting career. Mediocrity was the one thing I seemed capable of. The sheer melodrama of this feeling was disturbing. Richard had said I lived too intensely, and I began to think he was right. My emotions were pitched high, way up there with Saint Francis and his birds.

Then a centering thing happened: I heard Artur Rubinstein play Chopin at the Concertgebouw. He was eighty-six and long past the height of his powers, but he hadn't lost his magic. When he descended the red-carpeted stairs leading to the stage of the Grote Zaal, the audience rose as if for a king or a pope. Bowing stiffly, his cloud of white hair shining in the light, he looked, I thought, like a white rabbit in a tuxedo. It was clear he could no longer depend on brute virtuosity; he pulled the music together through deep understanding of its meaning and structure. His playing had—that word again—a rightness. He was still the Rubinstein I'd listened to and loved all my life. The concert left me in a state of unshakable tranquility.

I began playing Chopin at the Roodenburgs' upright piano, working on the easiest of the Nouvelles Études and a challenging but not-too-difficult C-sharp minor mazurka. It was a relief to be learning something again.

48

HILDE, ILSE, MANFRED, SCHNAPPS

I'D MANAGED TO WANGLE A BIT MORE money from my parents but was still on a tight leash when I took an eight-day trip to Innsbruck over Easter break. My father wanted me to see Innsbruck; it was where he'd gone to medical school, and he had good memories of the place. Mevrouw Roodenburg just wanted me out of the house. She didn't say so, but I could see she anticipated my absence with relief.

I took the fifteen-hour train ride with the one real friend I'd made in my class, a sociology major named Becky who was sweetly shy but trenchant and funny once I got to know her. Her mouth was scarred from, I assumed, a cleft-lip repair, but I'd never asked her about it. (I bristled when Mevrouw Roodenburg said, in that increasingly irritating high-pitched voice, "I feel sorry for her, her mouth.")

As we traveled south and started hearing German instead of Dutch, it was like buttoning myself into a stiff uniform after living in fatigues. I could no longer summon the conversational German I'd learned at school; the mere sound of the language made me feel like I was in enemy territory. That surprised me. But I knew we'd be welcomed once we got to Innsbruck. My brothers had been royally received there.

My father had lodged in a large, rambling house in the Kaiserjägerstrasse. His landlords were still living there: Hilde Ameseder, her husband, and her sister, Ilse Baur. A cousin ran a nearby hotel called the Grauer Bär, where Becky and I had arranged to stay. I expected it to be small and cozy, but it was huge and bustling. For a pittance, we were given a large, quiet room in the small guest house behind the hotel. Wonder of wonders, the bathroom had a stall shower. I hadn't had a proper shower since leaving Syracuse.

I'm describing the hotel because I have no words for its setting. The Tyrolean Alps were so—I'm about to say magnificent, breathtaking, and yes, they were, and the air was so clean and crisp I wanted to inhale and inhale it, though that could have been the unaccustomed altitude. The place had the sort of heart-stopping beauty that made me want to pretend I was a local and used to it. Becky said we ought to be spinning around like Julie Andrews in *The Sound of Music*, and she was right. I did not go so far as to buy a dirndl. I couldn't have afforded one. Even with our cheap room, it looked like we'd only have enough money for bread and cheese.

I should have known we could count on Hilde. She received me in an upstairs sitting room in that enormous house, a hefty woman in pants and a white smock, paintbrushes in hand. She was in her seventies and had disheveled auburn hair with white roots. Her face was very lined, her smile very gay. The large room was in elegant disarray, with several couches that might have served as beds, a cabinet full of dishes and silver, a coffee table with large chairs around it, a hotplate with a kettle. Tapestries—fabric collages, really—hung all about, the work of the prodigiously crafty Hilde, who clearly had a thing for the character Octavian in *Der Rosenkavalier*. And there was a wardrobe and a jewelry box and cabinets jammed full of god-knows-what. A person could have lived in that room for a month without needing anything except the kitchen next door—where, at the moment, a Turkish boy was painting decorations on urns for the family to sell. Hilde herself was redecorating a Tyrolese cabinet. Her dachshund, Poppea, raced about, barking for all she was worth. Hilde addressed her as "Poppylein," which is what I call my current cat.

Hilde served me instant coffee in eggshell-thin blue-and-white china, along with a marvelous coffee cake. And we talked—her English was excellent. She brought out photographs of my father as a med student. He looked like a boy, but he also hadn't changed: my father was one of those people who never seemed to age. He was relaxed and smiling in those photos, not at all the enigmatic, repressed man I knew. The Innsbruck years had been the happiest of his life, and after a short time in that house, I understood why. The food and drink and laughter never ceased. The family adored him. They called him Pepi, of all things, and spent innumerable raucous evenings together at the Grauer Bär. (Things got a bit awkward toward the end of his studies, just before the Anschluss. Someone in the household made a disparaging remark about Jews, then hastily added, "but *you're* okay, Pepi!")

I met Ilse, who looked older and frailer than Hilde and spoke no English. I tried speaking German with her but all I could produce was Dutch. It didn't matter. Like Hilde, she was overjoyed to see me. The uncanny thing was that I felt no need to present myself to these people in a careful way. I just talked—about my frustration with singing, my family, Amsterdam. The room began to fill with people I couldn't keep track of: Manfred, in his thirties and somebody's son, a jovial young doctor named Hermann, and three or four of their friends. We had vermouth, then wine, then little sandwiches with egg and mayonnaise and caviar, then soup with sausage-filled Tyrolese *knödel* the size of tennis balls. The conversation got sillier and sillier. We spent a fair amount of time demolishing the Dutch language. Then Hermann showed me how to drink schnapps. It was made from gentian and went down like fire and ice. He taught me how to say I was tipsy: *Ich habe einen Schwips*. The more I said it, the funnier it got.

He drove me back to the Grauer Bär in a Volkswagen with three of his friends, one of whom had his arm around my shoulder. Once again, I remembered Richard saying I didn't know how to have fun. I was having it now, with total strangers, in congenial confusion fueled by alcohol. There was an art to drinking oneself into giddy, unthinking oblivion. Furthermore, it was no bad thing. The language barrier helped; it freed me from my armor of words.

Hilde and Manfred took good care of us that week. There were excursions in the mountains and dinners in town. Becky and I did a fair amount of making like Julie Andrews and hiking in those glorious hills, where I learned what seemed an important lesson. I could see an enormous tree in an open field at the top of the first big hill. It looked like it was right in front of me, but to reach it, I had to walk far out of my way, taking detour after detour. The longest way round was the most direct.

49

STORMS

Mevrouw Roodenburg was displeased when I returned to Amsterdam the day after Easter. Didn't I know it was Second Easter, a holiday in the Netherlands? I did not. One more thing I'd gotten wrong. I'd noticed that my Dutch mother began an annoying number of sentences with, "In the Netherlands." She once told me that in the Netherlands, people were taught to play their piano pieces all the way through, not to work on one passage at a time. I knew this to be nonsense, but I also knew not to argue the point. She didn't like the way I practiced. Well, listening to someone practice can be tiresome.

Now she sat me down and told me I was too emotional, that I needed to learn to control myself because I was very hard to live with. I shared her little lecture with Mevrouw Citroen, who agreed I was far too emotional but didn't think I would be hard to live with. Perhaps that sort of family would have trouble living with someone of an artistic frame of mind, she said.

Out of context—away from the people I was used to, who were used to me—I had to come to a new reckoning of who I was and how I was seen by others. I made a list of things I thought the Roodenburgs thought I was: capricious, melancholy, frivolous, sedentary, wasteful, slothful, impulsive, brash, careless, clumsy, untidy, loud, abstruse, impractical, and unrealistic. I could see I was all those things—and that after a certain point, they would lose whatever quirky charm they might possess. So I resolved to be as quiet and unopinionated as possible in that home. To keep the peace.

I thought about the people in my life and realized I was what they saw me as—but that they didn't all see the same things. Not one of them knew about Ann Drummond-Grant, but surely, I was not the only person with a secret. I was . . . different. Unusual, in some as-yet-undetermined way. There was no fixing that, and I found I didn't mind it. Not knowing where my life was going was unnerving. But I didn't really mind that either.

Spring was in the air, sort of—the season couldn't make up its mind—and the semester would end in a matter of weeks. I wrote my father a long letter saying I wanted to stay in Amsterdam two more months to continue my studies with Mevrouw Citroen. It seemed terribly important, but by the time he had said yes, I'd grown tired of not having the money to pay her and being mercilessly lectured about my lack of discipline. I did not need yet another parent trying to whip me into shape. And the humming was getting me nowhere.

Some of my classmates were also staying on in Amsterdam, and one lived with a family that had an extra room for rent. The Storms were as irreverent as the Roodenburgs were reverent—we called them Moe and Pa, not Moeder and Vader. They were in their sixties, perhaps older, and had a house in the museum quarter. My room was at the very top, in the gable. It had an upright piano in reasonable tune and a radio that brought me the BBC. Hearing English—even endless unfollowable cricket matches—was a consolation. Since I listened almost exclusively to the classical music station, I heard no mention of the Watergate hearings. There were newspaper stories about "Waterkeet," but I didn't have enough Dutch to read them.

The Storms hosted several permanent lodgers in addition to the transient students, and together we made a family. There was Pa's favorite, a cultivated blind woman named Henriet; a woman named Gerda with a bad foot (Moe's favorite); a girl my age named Willy who had some kind of kidney problem; a timid young man named Luuk; and a procession of visiting friends and relatives. We would sit and eat and talk (in English and Dutch), and watch Pa boiling huge amounts of fruit into jam. It took discipline to run a household like that, but Pa and Moe were relaxed, and so were we. I fit right in. Everybody did.

I needed to find work to pay for voice lessons. But I soon decided I just wanted to earn money for presents for my friends at home. Moe knew of an organization of volunteers through which someone without a work permit (like me) could make a little cash helping people who were sick or disabled. The first woman I worked for had MS and reminded me so much of my mother that I kept dropping and breaking things. But the second, who had six children and was recovering from a hysterectomy, was so cheerful and easygoing that I enjoyed cleaning for her. Even ironing.

I didn't make a formal break with Mevrouw Citroen; I just let the lessons peter out. So I was shocked to encounter her in Paris, where I spent a weekend with a classmate. We shared a squalid hotel room and lived on bread and cheese and cheap wine. Of course we got around via the Metro, the truest Underworld this side of the River Styx. It was in one of those deep labyrinthine passageways that I saw Mevrouw Citroen—my personal Fury—playing the accordion to earn a few francs. But no: it was her doppelgänger. I drew closer and saw that this woman was blind, with eyes that stared in different directions. Her smile gave me chills.

50

SCORPIO

I SPENT DECADES WONDERING WHEN Ann Drummond-Grant's birthday was—it was tiresome knowing only the day she died. But no source gave it; nobody seemed to know. I was over fifty when I finally visited the General Register Office in Edinburgh in search of her birth record. The helpful lady there was unable to unearth any trace of her. Was I quite sure she was legitimate? Well, I *thought* she was. And there didn't seem to be any illegitimate births that fit the bill. Finally it occurred to me to drop the hyphen, and that was the magic key: She was Annie D. Grant, named after her grandmother who was born Ann Drummond and married Robert Grant.

In Britain in those days, double-barreled names smacked of aristocracy, but I don't believe Drummie had it in her to pretend she was posh. I believe that, as a serious young singer with high aspirations, she was not about to present herself to the world as Annie Grant—a name that sounds like it belongs in a music hall—or as plain, dour Ann Grant. The hyphen might have been for clarity. Without it, "Drummond" would have looked like a maiden name.

She was born at 8:00 p.m. on November 20, 1904. Once I knew this, I did an obsessive thing: I commissioned a reading from an astrologer. It seemed a logical way of bonding, girlfriend to girlfriend, Gemini to Scorpio, with the powerful woman who'd loomed over me for so long.

Okay. There were three astrologers. I commissioned readings from all of them.

I didn't tell them anything about Drummie, other than the time and place of her birth. But they all saw things in her chart that I know to be true: that she had an overwhelming need to express herself creatively and was driven to achieve this through intense discipline and commitment. That she was a perfectionist who focused more on what she got wrong than what she got right. That she had a fine mind and a dark sense of humor that not everybody got. That she lived a public life, surrounded by people, yet seemed somehow solitary.

She was very much a Scorpio, one astrologer said, and Scorpio is a powerful, willful sign, a sign of struggle and transformation, a catalyst for others. She had Cancer rising, like me. If she and I had been friends, she wouldn't have let me get away with being less than my best, and I would have wanted to inspire her as much as she inspired me. It would have been intense. Hell, it *has* been intense.

The astrologers all said that Drummie had a difficult childhood in which she raged against some struggle or conflict. Her mother had an infirmity that forced Drummie to become the caretaker, said one. There was instability related to her father, who undermined the family in some way—he was weak or emotionally unavailable or a poor provider. And there were cultural or religious expectations that led her to sacrifice herself for her family's sake.

I didn't need an astrologer to tell me any of this. I could connect the dots from the public record: Drummie's mother had a damaged heart and died young. Her father, a traveling salesman, was absent a lot, and there was no money for household help. Drummie and her sister were teenagers when their mother died, and in Edinburgh at that time, there would have been enormous pressure on them to conform—to be good girls, care for their widowed father, and, in due course, find husbands and produce children. Those expectations ran entirely counter to Drummie's consuming desire to forge a career onstage. But she stuck it out at home for fifteen years: eleven years till her father died, then four more years till Agnes married. Considering the scope of her ambition and talent, she was a genie trapped in a bottle.

Once she left home and began her career in earnest, she took up with a married man—a Jew, for heaven's sake—and lived with him out of wedlock. From the perspective of my time, this was simply the liberated thing to do, but it was clearly not the conduct of the kind of woman she'd been raised to become. I feel sure she paid an emotional price for the choices she made.

Drummie knew what she wanted, which is rare enough. She knew she had an exceptional voice and worked like a fiend to do it justice, though her upbringing compelled her to present a modest face to the world. She cast her lot, decisively, with the man she fell in love with—but there must have been nights when she lay awake wondering if their sinful relationship would send her to hell. This was a woman who simultaneously freed and imprisoned herself.

I see I've just described an experience of being female.

51

TWO CONTRALTOS, 1950

DRUMMIE'S FATHER TRAVELED FOR A LIVING, and she took a husband who did the same. She and Goddie spent significant time apart during the war. Afterward, she pursued her career, and he pursued his. I know, for example, that starting in 1949, she toured for eleven long months in a musical called *Waltzes From Vienna*. By then, her voice had deepened enough for her to approach the contralto roles in G&S, raising the possibility that she and her husband could work together. It must have seemed the best of all possible worlds.

But she didn't just swan back into the D'Oyly Carte. According to Tony Joseph's history of the company, "she begged to be allowed to return . . . even if only as a chorister." Which she did, in August 1950. It's not clear whether she actually performed in the chorus, but she occasionally went on as understudy to the company's redoubtable contralto, Ella Halman. She also sang the soubrette roles—Iolanthe, Mad Margaret, Phoebe—on the recordings I fell in love with. At forty-six, she was too old in every way to play those roles. But if she hadn't recorded them, imprinting all her passion and power in that vinyl, I might not have heard her urgent call. She was singing to *me*.

At this point, she was literally waiting in the wings to take over Ella Halman's roles, and I gather this was not okay with Ella. Quite a lot was not okay in the ranks of the D'Oyly Carte. At the end of the 1950–51 season, twenty-seven people left the company. Five principals were among them, including Halman and the company's biggest star, Martyn Green. At least some of them quit in frustration at how they were treated by management.

The rift had been growing since 1948, when Rupert D'Oyly Carte died and his daughter, Bridget, took over. In his memoir, Green is more coy than candid about the reasons for the general discontent, but it's clear he puts the bulk of the blame on Miss Bridget. As Hans Conried told me, he thought she was a dragon lady.

Bridget D'Oyly Carte could be distant and imperious, calling the shots from her aerie in the world's fanciest hotel. Some of her decisions were deeply misguided—most notably, the appointment (from the chorus) of a director of productions who was in no way qualified for the job. That was the last straw for many. But Miss Bridget, buttoned-up elitist though she was, cared deeply about the company. To the end. And the D'Oyly Carte was what it was: blithely, fearlessly, fatally resistant to change.

Martyn Green was a superb performer, and I can see why he felt angry at not being listened to. "It is apparently assumed . . . that the performers are little more than automatons," he wrote. "Production is done to a plan that takes no consideration of the individual, his personality, or his histrionic ability—a stereotyped plan that results in a clockwork performance devoid of spontaneity." There's truth in this. D'Oyly Carte performances were reliably good and reliably uniform, with a consistency both admired and bemoaned. But there was simply no other way to run a touring company that churned out eight performances a week, forty-eight weeks a year. If one player got sick or left the company, another had to be plugged in.

Which leads me to a rumor I suspect is true: that Ella Halman finally decided she was done with the D'Oyly Carte on the day she arrived early for a rehearsal and discovered Ann Drummond-Grant running through *her* part with Isidore Godfrey. Ella was not amused. Nor would I have been. It would be like catching your husband with his next wife—in this case, his actual wife. This is gossip, of course. What the public saw was a fairly orderly changing of the guard, with the new principals eventually deemed to be as strong as the old ones—though the old ones were never forgotten. When Drummie took over the contralto roles, she was compared to every contralto who'd gone before her: Ella Halman, Evelyn Gardiner, Dorothy Gill, and, for people with very long memories, the great Bertha Lewis. I can see them in their costumes as I write their names.

I don't have all their voices in my head, but I do have Ella's. She was a true contralto with a dark, rich sound, markedly different from Drummie's powerful mezzo, which could plumb the depths of the contralto register but never lost its shining top. For the purposes of the D'Oyly Carte, what mattered was that both women could sing the roles, had strong constitutions and good comic timing, and were of appropriate height and heft to act as foils to the comic baritones.

There was never a question that Drummie's status as the wife of the musical director had any bearing on her winning those roles. Nor did she receive special treatment from him: in rehearsals, he addressed her as "Miss Grant." She worked as hard as anyone—arguably harder than most, since the contralto appeared in every opera and never got a night off. She became a favorite, a stalwart, a star, but that entailed still more work: being gracious to fans, signing endless autographs, writing endless thank-you notes in her unfailingly clear hand—and on tour, being mustered for press appearances (like that radio interview in San Francisco) instead of sightseeing or sleeping in.

She rose to it all without the slightest display of temperament or ego. Tony Joseph, who was in his teens in the 1950s, remembered her chatting to fans outside the stage door: "This tall, gentle mother- or aunt-like figure dressed in a thick coat, usually wearing a hat, with Godfrey in tow looking almost short beside her, holding the lead at the other end of which was their little dog." The dog was a Cairn terrier called Dougal. Drummie loved dogs.

"I think in her quiet way, she was a warm person, capable of arousing great affection, with a soft voice that still contained a trace of her Scottish accent—the rolling r's in particular—and I remember how distressed I felt when she died." Tony wrote this to me in an email some years ago. It was the first time I had heard her described as quiet or gentle, my first inkling of who she was offstage. In my own life, she was a thunderbolt, a "mighty protectress" like the Fairy Queen in *Iolanthe*. But to her colleagues in the company, and to the larger community of D'Oyly Carte followers and fans, she was family. With each new memoir, each letter, each scrap of audio that emerges from this community, I get another glimpse of her, and every glimpse feels like a little visitation: she and I continue to meet in unexpected places. But I will not claim to know her. I'm not sure I could know her, even if we'd shared a stage or a dressing room. Wherever I meet her, there's a stillness, a secrecy. And that peerless, dignified sadness.

52

THE JOB

HAVING PERFORMED EXACTLY ONE QUASI-OPERATIC role for exactly two nights in a high school auditorium, I can't begin to comprehend what it meant to work as hard as Drummie did— to perform night after night in theater after theater, somehow getting enough rest to keep the voice in shape. To maintain the same impeccable standard for each new audience. To make those battleaxe roles her own.

There's a famous quote about her from Darrell Fancourt, who sang the bass-baritone roles, thrillingly, for more than thirty years (and who was a witness at her wedding). Ann Drummond-Grant, he said, was "one of the very few people who have sung the contralto parts in Gilbert and Sullivan not as hard, *beastly* women but with a true understanding of their light and shade." I've long sensed that she inhabited the liminal space between light and darkness. Not one or the other, but both.

Drummie performed eight contralto roles but lived to record only three: Katisha in *The Mikado*, Ruth in *Pirates*, and Lady Blanche in *Princess Ida*. She also recorded a ninth role, Lady Sangazure, in *The Sorcerer*, an opera that wasn't in the repertoire. The first Lady Sangazure had a deep voice, and her part lies very low, almost too low for comfort. Drummie had sung the soprano role, which is quite high, in the 1930s. Back then, she would have been coached to speak her lines in a high-pitched, girlish register. As a contralto, she'd have spoken them at least an octave lower, in a rich, booming voice. It was how all D'Oyly Carte contraltos spoke.

I first heard that subterranean speaking voice only recently, when two BBC broadcasts from the fifties came to light. They're amateur recordings lifted from the radio, so the sound isn't brilliant. But I love them because they're live, with a responding audience. One is *The Mikado*, where I can hear not just her thrilling entrance as Katisha but the *whap!* of her heavy kimono sleeves as she wheels around to confront the chorus. The other is *The Gondoliers*, a particular gift because it contains one of the roles she didn't record, the Duchess of Plaza Toro.

The duchess is the only one of Gilbert's contraltos to have a husband, the henpecked duke. The two of them have no source of income other than what they can swindle out of others, but they're extremely good at it. I used to stare at photos of Drummie standing regally in her duchess costumes, reflexively straightening my own spine. But her duchess is *funny*. With perfect timing, she wrings every bit of tart humor from the part. Her singing voice, as always, is glorious—open, free, and absolutely at her command. Which is remarkable, since at the time of this broadcast, in January 1959, she was probably dealing with considerable pain.

But then, she was known for her absolute reliability onstage. If someone had a momentary lapse and got tangled in Gilbert's thickets of words, throwing the other cast members off—it happened more often than you might think, in complicated ensembles with multiple refrains—Drummie never lost her place. Tony Joseph writes about a time when the lights went out while she, as the duchess, was singing a duet with Peter Pratt's duke: "The blackout, [Pratt] admitted, all but finished *him*. By contrast, she kept going quite untroubled, missing not a word or a note throughout."

The orchestra kept going, too—even though, according to Goddie, not all the players knew the score well enough to continue in darkness: "I had to shout cues to the local musicians who had joined us for our stay in that town."

It's obvious that he and Drummie were made for each other.

Because of the relentless work and the constant touring that flung them all together for months at a time—on trains and ocean liners, in digs and hotels, in theaters that were alternately chilly or stifling but inevitably dusty—the company was exceptionally close-knit. They lived their lives on the road, taking their hobbies with them: golf, tennis, cricket, oil painting, basket weaving, marquetry(!), every kind of needlework. During the seven months of the 1955 tour, they saw more of North America than I ever will, most of it by rail. In Central City, Colorado, they sang at nine thousand feet above sea level, which isn't easy. In Los Angeles, they applied oil-based makeup in sweltering dressing rooms during a heat wave where temperatures reached 120 degrees Fahrenheit. It was bitterly cold in Toronto, but Montreal was even colder: twenty below zero. Those who had the occasional performance off (i.e., not Goddie or Drummie) saw every sight there was to see. It was, for all of them, the tour of a lifetime.

I have a group photo from the beginning of that tour, in Central City. Everyone is impeccably attired, the men in suits and ties, the women in crisp dresses. D'Oyly Carters were expected to dress to the nines at all times. Drummie smiles serenely, looking utterly relaxed. When photographed in costume, she always assumed the attitude of her character. But here, in a patterned, perfectly pressed cotton dress, she's happy to be who she is, where she is.

Toward the end of the tour, in New York, one of the dressers, a trained nurse, told a company member she was concerned that "Miss Grant might be unwell."

53

HOT BLACK

Cynthia Morey writes that Ann Drummond-Grant was "a Grande Dame—she had wonderful stage presence, and when she made an entrance, no one was left in any doubt that somebody important had arrived." An American newspaper critic dubbed her "Ann Drum and Bugle" because of the way she rallied the cast around her.

She had presence offstage too, and there were those who found her intimidating. Kenneth Sandford, who sang the heavier baritone roles, alluded in his memoir to her "dowager austerity." Jeffrey Skitch, who sang the lighter baritone parts, told me in an email that she could be standoffish: "Drummie was a Scottish lady, and they are sometimes a little reserved, at least to English eyes."

Skitch, I think, didn't quite get her. He definitely didn't get what Morey calls her "lugubrious" sense of humor. "She could certainly see the funny side of things—even when not everyone thought it funny," he wrote. "An example of this—driving in wintertime from Stratford to Harrogate, my car slowly skidded off the road and smashed its nearside front wheel. I was able to put on the spare. . . . The next day, Drummie thought the whole thing was quite amusing. I didn't!"

I suppose this incident really wasn't what you'd call funny. But when Skitch wrote to me fifty years after the fact, he was still fuming about being laughed at. I can see the humor in that.

It may have been her younger female colleagues who saw more of Drummie's nurturing side. To them, she was something of a den mother, watching from the wings to give them moral support, coaching them in their dialogue, warning them of pitfalls, and helping them make the most of their parts. They were grateful: newcomers received no such help from management. It was up to the old hands to show them the ropes.

Morey writes that it was Drummie who showed her how to use "hot black," a waxy paste that got heated in a spoon over a candle and applied, drop by drop, to the eyelashes. Applying the stuff required Zen-like patience and concentration, but Drummie always used it, building up her lashes till they were an eighth of an inch thick. "I often wondered how she managed to open her eyes," said Jon Ellison, a colleague who was no slouch at makeup himself. Elli was with the company for many years, playing small baritone roles and understudying larger ones. He wrote me a wonderful letter about her, and I need to let him speak.

I first met Drummie on 3 September 1953 during my first full company rehearsal with D'Oyly Carte. I was a little wet behind the ears, having joined the Company only two days previously, after completing my two years National Service with the Army.

I remember very clearly this statuesque lady approaching me on the stage of the Savoy Theatre, where we were rehearsing prior to going on tour. She advanced towards me and proffered her hand, whilst wishing me a happy time with the Company in a refined Edinburgh accent. I said that I was a little apprehensive, to which she replied, "Och, awa wi' ye!" and gave her familiar, deliciously warm laugh.

In the years I worked alongside her I never saw or heard her give a poor performance. She was always 100 percent plus! Her wonderful first entrance as Katisha in *Mikado* was electrifying, and it was quite impossible not to respond to her.

I loved her in everything she did. Her Lady Jane in *Patience* was a dream—I never failed to be convulsed by her Act II opening with her gloriously overdone mock-cello playing. [Jane "accompanies" herself on a cello.] She used the bow as if she were sawing a log—glorious! Her Fairy Queen in *Iolanthe* was so gracefully regal—beautiful hand movements, worthy of a star ballerina. And what a tyrant she was as the Duchess in *Gondoliers*. . . .

There's no way I will ever see those bits of stage business. I had so little of her, really. But it felt like everything.

There's a lovely photo of Drummie coming offstage as Lady Jane with the cello slung over her shoulder, greeting the stage manager with a warm, open smile. It was Jon Ellison who told me that her eyes were blue. (I'd seen her only in black and white.) "On many occasions they had a little saucy twinkle," he wrote. "When she was very happy, they would dance."

It was also Jon who told me about that time she had a nasty cold and croaked on a single note, "so little, I doubt if anyone in the audience was aware it had happened. However, when she came off into the wings after the scene, she was desperately upset and close to tears."

She was terribly hard on herself. As I said, her discipline ran deep. In the San Francisco radio interview, she spoke in her low, lilting way about the need for constant rehearsal: "The producer might say to you, such and such a thing is not as *crisp* or as *good* as it has been, and that makes you think—well, maybe not. Even to be *told* that rather, you know, jerks you up—and you think: well, I must concentrate and get that back to perfection again. When you play roles for a long time, you can get a little *mechanical* if you don't just keep absolutely into the character."

That was the challenge for everyone in the company: performing the same roles over and over and finding fresh joy in them.

Backstage, says Jon Ellison, Drummie "was very natural and relaxed, and would always have a word to say to us minions, but she did like a brief few minutes' peace just prior to her entrances, and on occasion I have seen her running through sections of dialogue to herself. Then, on her entrance cue, she would visibly change, and would no longer be Drummie but the Fairy Queen. . . ."

That's what performers do. It describes every real performer I've known. Discipline is what carries you. Discipline is delight. For Drummie, eternally on the road, discipline was home. As Jon Ellison tells it, even her little dog was disciplined. (This isn't surprising, since Drummie had spent at least one summer as a teenager on her uncle's livestock farm and knew what a well-trained dog could do.)

> Dougal went everywhere with her. He would come into the theatre with her and go straight to her dressing room. He had visited so many theatres on so many occasions that he knew exactly where to go. She had special dispensations for him to spend the performances in her dressing rooms. Dogs in dressing rooms were frowned upon, but he was very well-behaved and never made a sound until the final curtain, when he seemed to sense that it was all over, and the corridors would resound to his excited barking.

Dougal was very much a one-woman dog. After Drummie died, he continued to tour with Goddie and spent the performances in the musical director's dressing room. I feel he was very important to Goddie and kept Drummie's memory alive.

54

CONSCIOUSNESS, 1973

COMING HOME FROM AMSTERDAM AFTER six months was every bit as disorienting as arriving there. My father picked me up at JFK and immediately made the five-hour drive to Syracuse. Back in February, he'd driven through a snowstorm to get me to the airport. Now, in August, the air was warm and heavy with humidity. The roadside greenery seemed lush and overgrown to the point of decadence; all the cars looked indecently huge. Holland had been small and orderly. This place was the opposite.

I don't believe he and I talked much during that drive. He knew enough not to bombard me with questions I would be disinclined to answer. We had an understanding that the two of us were on the same wavelength, no matter what. At least he thought so.

It was midnight when we got home. There was Mother and Mother's house—her turf—where I was not eager to be. How she felt about my return I couldn't say. The rooms looked strange and unwelcoming, and I was too tired to make peace with them or with her. So I laced my speech with Dutch words I knew she couldn't understand. "Do you think I have *dikke benen?*" I asked as I undressed for bed. *Do you think I have fat legs?* I looked down and saw that they were certainly hairy, and flabby too. Home was where I hated my body.

I knew even in my jet-lagged stupor that things would have to change, that I couldn't resume the life I'd left six months before. I was done with the idea of becoming an actress. I didn't want to be in Syracuse. Music was what I was passionate about, and I would find a better place to study singing. I would take a few music courses at SU, then transfer to a real conservatory at the end of the fall semester. I would not return to Miss Pinnell.

There remained the problem of choosing that real conservatory and getting into it. And of finding a teacher who could prepare me for the audition. But first, *mirabile dictu*, there was the prospect of returning to Lake Placid, where Starker and Sebök were once again giving master classes.

The two of them played just one recital that week, and I arrived in the middle of it, having snagged a ride at the last minute. They were playing Bach in a small dark hall, lit only by the acid glow of a yellow spotlight that made their white jackets vibrate. The strange illumination pulled them out of time: it was Now, and Now was Bach. I was last in line to greet them after the concert, clutching a white flower and feeling very shy. Sebök, exhausted from playing in Connecticut one night and Schroon Lake the next, looked at me with bloodshot eyes and was silent for a long moment. His face lit slowly, incredulously, and he opened his arms in amazed welcome.

"How *are* you?"

I could only smile.

"*Vere* are you?" That musical Hungarian accent. "I thought you were in Europe! Are you acting?"

It amazes me to this day that he remembered who I was and was glad to see me. I'd written to him twice and gotten prompt replies; he knew I was studying acting. But the signal thing about Sebök was that he actually paid attention. I felt I was being acknowledged as an adult human being for the first time in ages. We kissed each other's cheeks.

That week, once more, I scribbled away in my notebook, racing to capture everything he said. Once more, I marveled at how he taught on several levels at once, addressing the physicality of piano technique, the emotional response of the pianist—and hence, the listener—to the music, and the thought processes that brought it all together. Body, mind, emotions, and something more: consciousness. Sebök was deeply interested in consciousness. I might even say he was obsessed with it, but the obsession was matter-of-fact. He taught the whole student because he saw the whole student, relating to people at what he perceived to be their level of awareness. Consciousness, he said, was a dangerous thing—and so was teaching.

I asked him what he meant by this one evening at a party where people were drinking wine from paper cups and talking louder and louder. (Who actually enjoys that sort of party?) We conversed in fits and starts, holding our thoughts between interruptions. He mentioned the teachings of Gurdjieff, whom I'd never heard of. Most people, he said, are at least partly asleep most of the time. I knew that feeling. There were whole days when I felt myself moving through life as though I were painted onto its surface. Gurdjieff, Sebök said, talked about a higher state of consciousness which a human being might possibly attain: "Once I think I reached it, and for a few moments I knew *everything*." He smiled. "I have forgotten it."

He said it so casually. It was the first time anyone had told me firsthand about such an experience. I thought it was what Liszt was trying to describe in his piece about Saint Francis and the birds—Liszt who gazed heavenward as he played and made women swoon. (Sebök collected photos of Liszt.) Gazing heavenward appealed to me, though Sebök said that in performance it was *cabotinage*, deliberate and useful theatricality. A performance is the product of so much practice that even the sublime moments are premeditated.

Consciousness, too, must be practiced, but I didn't know that; I had no idea discipline was involved. I'd never read about the Buddhist concept of enlightenment, or tried to meditate, or sought to untangle myself through therapy. Such things were not yet fashionable. I knew people who'd taken LSD and swore it was an expressway to awareness, but it looked dangerously random to me. In Amsterdam, I had encountered Hare Krishnas and Jesus freaks. *Take up the finger cymbals and find your bliss! Take Jesus into your heart and never worry again!* Lost souls looking for a shortcut, I thought with more than a little contempt.

I knew it mattered that I be present for my own life—and I wasn't. I knew music could take me out of myself, but I didn't know what that self was. I thought I was brilliant at charming small talk but knew the brilliance to be a mask. Sebök didn't even try to make small talk; he said he was no good at it. Nor did he try to hide the deep sadness in his eyes. He presented himself as he was.

It was one of those cold, dazzlingly clear Adirondack summer nights. I went outside and saw a meteor streak across a sky crammed full of stars. I came back in and reported this to Sebök, who said, "Without *me?*" I thought he was teasing, but he said, "No, I mean it. I always feel cheated if something cosmic happens and I'm not there."

He invariably wanted to be there. One night, a pack of us stumbled down a pitch-dark path to see the stars reflected in the lake, our way lit only by the tiny flame of his cigarette lighter. (How could he smoke at such a time? He couldn't *not* smoke.) Stars upon stars upon stars. Unearthly silence, broken by the calls of a distant loon and the occasional hiss of a cigarette thrown into the water. It was one of the best conversations we had: no conversation at all.

I did play for him that week: the C-sharp minor Chopin mazurka I'd learned in Amsterdam. I acquitted myself decently, though I discovered there were basic things I didn't understand about it. A mazurka is a dance with three beats to a measure, but the accents are fluid; there are passages where the third beat is accented because, Sebők said, that's where the dancer's foot hits the floor. Once more I was reminded that music begins in the body.

Music, as Sebők taught it, involved trying to feel what the composer felt. Why, he asked, did Beethoven mark a passage *crescendo*? He wanted it to get louder, obviously, but "louder" is not a feeling. A pianist needs to find the emotion behind that marking, the inner tension that builds the crescendo. Learning to do this is as much a part of piano technique as mastering scales and arpeggios. Body, mind, emotions, *consciousness*. The deeper your understanding of a piece of music, the closer it brings you to—no, not the sublime heavenward gaze. Not at all. The greatness of great music lies in the composer's humanity, revealed as miraculous.

55

A DECISION

Fast forward to Fred Marvin's piano class a few months later. Fred preferred classes to individual lessons; he said it was the European way. This was a marathon session to make up for the week off he'd taken before his recital at Crouse, where I'd found his playing tentative. Now, at least ten of us fought drowsiness in the stained-glass haze of his living room—the Church of Fred—with its German Steinways, oriental rugs, deep soft couches, and innumerable *objets*. On an antique table by the fireplace, next to a magenta hibiscus and a swaybacked brass Buddha, an incense burner emitted clouds of overpowering musk. Anyone who sat near it would start choking and have to move. I was across the room and still felt dizzy.

Fred wore a wine-colored silk smoking jacket, the first such garment I'd seen in active use. I think he was trying to create an aura of elegant informality, but he only reminded me of Bunthorne, the charlatan poet in *Patience*. One after the other, we roused ourselves from our torpor and played for him. Students who'd been with me in Sebök's master classes, where they'd been heard with respect, were made to play single passages over and over again in search of tiny nuances, all of which were Fred's. By now, I knew the futility of approaching a piece of music one measure at a time. All it yielded, if you were lucky, was a series of manicured phrases.

That last semester at Syracuse, I saw little of Fred, who went off to Europe to concertize. I prepared for my piano jury on my own, practicing Bach's Chromatic Fantasia and Fugue on the instrument my parents had bought in an unsolicited show of support, a Mason & Hamlin grand built in 1914. Its once-shiny finish was a mess of black flakes, but it was a serious instrument with a nice action and a beautiful, mellow sound. Lucille Sack, consulted on the purchase, had approved, saying, "It's built like a brick shithouse." Playing that piano was the one good thing about living at home, the one scrap of turf that was truly mine. I still have it. It's been refinished, refurbished, and carted to multiple dwellings, all 850 pounds of it.

But my main task was getting into a conservatory as a voice major. As usual, brute intuition took the place of research. I told myself I wanted a school in a real city, not some university town. I didn't even think of applying to Juilliard, knowing full well I couldn't get in. The Manhattan School of Music sounded impressive, and so did the New England Conservatory in Boston. Why not one of those? Lucille seemed to think they were good options, so I sent away for catalogs. The Manhattan School sent theirs in a hot minute. New England's took weeks to arrive—by which time I'd already scheduled an audition at Manhattan. And that, really truly, is how I made one of the more momentous decisions of my life: cavalierly, with a dart flung backward over my left shoulder. I almost didn't care. I just wanted to get on with it.

I needed help with the audition. Lucille had one of her brain waves and set me up with Victoria Beach, a mezzo-soprano with one of those big, lush voices that make you forget everything else. She lived around the corner in a grand, orderly house—from the 1920s, like my parents' house, but built for people with money. She'd never had a voice student. But she knew what good singing was; she understood registration, placement, breath support. Marilyn Horne was her idol. Listen to her, she said, if you want to hear what a great singer can do.

Mrs. Beach couldn't have done much for my technique in those few months, but she boosted my confidence. Of *course* I'd get into a conservatory! Yes, I had a young instrument, but I was brimming with potential, and *so* musical. "You were *born* to sing!" she said, her resonant voice enveloping me like a motherly hug. She had four children, and her motherliness was something to bask in.

I wasn't at all sure I was born to sing. But it helped that Mrs. Beach thought I was.

She seemed fascinated that I'd attained the great age of twenty without ever having a boyfriend. (I must have told her this. She must have asked.) One morning in the middle of a lesson, she said, out of nowhere: "You know, men just *need* sex. Like they need that morning cup of coffee." And suddenly I was imagining this large, regal woman enfolding her handsome lawyer husband in an obliging embrace. It was a piece of information I didn't know what to do with.

Mrs. Beach did teach me some useful things about singing. The simple Italian songs I disdained as being for beginners were in fact a key to vocal mastery. With their legato lines and open vowels, she said, they were medicine for the voice. It was she who finally made me understand that vowels carry the sound of the voice, while consonants are interruptions that must be kept as short as possible.

If I'd grown up listening to grand opera rather than Gilbert and Sullivan, I might have understood this better. Some D'Oyly Carte principals, Ann Drummond-Grant being one, were superbly trained singers with operatic voices. Others were decently trained singers with decent voices, compensating for their vocal shortcomings with charisma and charm. They were theater people: entertainers first, singers second. Opera singers are singers first, last, and always. Nowadays they also have to be able to act, but the voice is still paramount.

Mrs. Beach had me prepare Mimi's first aria from *La Bohème*. I was thrilled that she thought I was ready for it, but in truth, I wasn't. I'd heard *Bohème* on the radio and seen a local production. Yet I didn't understand the signal thing about Puccini's consumptive heroine, which is that, fragile as she is, she's a lyric soprano with a spine of steel. Her voice must have substance; it has to bloom in the middle, not just at the top. I might have been able to approach Musetta's Waltz from the same opera, which lies higher. But I probably wasn't ready for that either.

Did I understand what Mimi was singing, and why? Sort of, but that wasn't the issue. Most of her aria lay smack in the middle of my range, where the problems were, and the climactic high notes weren't all that high. But it was my showpiece. I planned to work up to it with an art song or two, stuff I really did know how to sing. The audition didn't go that way.

56

MANHATTAN

EARLY NOVEMBER 1973: NEW YORK at its seediest, most dysfunctional, and most dangerous. My father arranged for me to stay with one of his old medical school classmates who lived on the Upper West Side with his wife and daughter. They had one of those rambling prewar apartments that make the city seem quiet and civilized. On the day of my audition, the daughter, whose name was Pearl, walked me to the subway at 79th and Broadway, where a deranged homeless man, filthy and half naked, was pacing and ranting. "Pay no attention to him," she said. "He's just a New York Crazy." The audition was at 122nd and Broadway. Pearl had me get off the train at 116th Street rather than 125th, which she deemed unsafe.

The Manhattan School of Music was in the building formerly occupied by the Juilliard School, which had recently moved downtown to Lincoln Center. "JUILLIARD" was still carved into the limestone on the Broadway side. A second-hand building for a second-tier school, I thought, suitable for a second-rate singer. But it was an elegant structure, built in 1910 and expanded in the 1930s, with a new glass pavilion where students gathered to eat and talk. I took it all in with no thought for the deep-pocketed donors who had made the place possible. It was grand in its quiet way, sitting at the north end of an academic neighborhood that was home to Columbia

University, Barnard College, and the Union and Jewish Theological Seminaries. It also abutted Spanish Harlem, where nobody's pockets were deep.

The audition was held in a small, perfectly proportioned recital hall, where a capable accompanist waited at a Steinway grand. I felt comfortable on that stage, looking down at the encouraging smiles of the voice faculty, and was about to begin with a Fauré chanson when I was stopped by a man with an authoritative voice, who said, "Are you up to starting with the Mimi?" I knew I wasn't. I needed to be thoroughly warmed up and to take the measure of my voice in that space, in order to give Mimi's aria my best shot. But I couldn't imagine saying no to him, so I nodded yes.

The authoritative man was Daniel Ferro, head of the voice faculty. I later learned he was always on the lookout for big voices that could be groomed for operatic careers. He would have known within ten seconds that mine wasn't one of them. I got through the aria as best I could, with frazzled nerves and a threadbare voice. I don't even remember if I got to sing a second number. Perhaps I did. A sense of failure took hold of me and didn't let go. I'd blown it.

Afterward, in shock, I sat on a folding chair outside the recital hall and sobbed. I didn't know how I could face another human being. A tall man with graying hair walked by and, seeing me in that state, asked what had happened. He might have guessed, knowing that auditions were going on. I told him everything, total stranger that he was: how I was auditioning as a transfer student, had been asked to start cold with the wrong piece, and had sung it badly. He didn't actually say, "There, there," but he managed to comfort me. He knew how it felt to mangle an audition, he said—it happened to everyone. He was the director of admissions, and he would see what he could do.

This encounter left me in a different kind of shock. The tall, kindly man was a deus ex machina swooping in to rescue me—a sign, surely, that Ann Drummond-Grant was watching over me, nudging events into place.

Well . . . no. It was a fortunate meeting, but the truth was I needn't have worried. The Manhattan School of Music was happy to accept me as a voice major, provided I was willing to start over as a freshman and pay four more years of tuition. Some of my SU credits would be transferred, but not the vocal ones. My parents weren't thrilled, but they acquiesced. I saw it as a fresh start. I still had hope that my voice could grow.

I was disabused of that notion at the beginning of the spring semester, when I was assigned a voice teacher named Suzanne Sten-Taubman. (I had no choice in the matter.) There was a hierarchy among students and teachers, and none of the better students studied with her. She'd taught exactly one singer with a major career. The rest of her students were people like me who had so-so voices but brought in tuition dollars. There were any number of us at MSM. I used to wonder what the others were doing there. I was getting the damn degree.

Miss Sten-Taubman was a mezzo-soprano in her midsixties. She'd had an operatic career in Europe in the thirties before emigrating with her late husband, the accompanist Leo Taubman. (Before fleeing, I mean. They were Jews.) By the time I met her, all that remained of her voice was a resonant hoot, but she sang gorgeously on a 1940 recording of one of Mahler's Rückert-Lieder. She knew something, in other words. And tried to impart it to me. But the best she could do was to tell me to produce the tone and "just set it." Set it on the breath, I think she meant. I sang a lot of Bach with her and struggled with it. Bach wrote for the voice the way he wrote for wind instruments, and his long, fluid lines require the kind of breath support I didn't understand.

She was kind, though. It can't have been easy to teach me; I had been cloaked in hopelessness when I walked into her studio. Damaged goods. There were many things I did right as a singer. I sang in tune, shaped phrases beautifully, enunciated (too) clearly in several languages, breathed in the right places, conveyed the dramatic arc of a song. I had excellent stage presence, stood tall, cast the right kind of spell. The one thing I didn't have was proper command of my physical instrument. Someone should have taught me that. Someone eventually did, but not while I was in music school. All I knew, every time I opened my mouth, was that my voice didn't measure up.

But I worked diligently, improving just enough to avoid despair. I was in a real conservatory now, with talent all around me. The most gifted singers studied with Daniel Ferro (who never spoke to me after my audition) or one of the other big names like Rose Bampton or Ellen Faull, but there were a lot of good teachers on that voice faculty, and quite a few good students too.

The thing was, even the best voices were works in progress. My classmates were kids with stars in their eyes. I became acutely aware that there were no stars in mine. Yes, I was two years older than they were. But that wasn't it. How do I put this? They cared about *singing* a lot more than I did. They loved opera, lieder, oratorio. Broadway. Jazz and pop. They listened passionately to all kinds of singers and wanted more than anything to perform, singing snatches of arias at the slightest provocation. I had to face the realization that this wasn't me.

I had elevated one singer above all others, and I loved that dead artist more than the living art. My dream of performing had been specific to the D'Oyly Carte. When the dream wavered, no other took its place. I never fantasized about taking bows before an adoring audience—I couldn't imagine singing well enough to be adored. Yet I was majoring in vocal performance, with the supposed intent of making a living as a singer. And I'd just committed myself to four more years of study. So I simply put off thinking about the future. "Fiddle-dee-dee," said Scarlett O'Hara. "I'll think about that tomorrow."

57

CLAREMONT AVE.

Besides, I was in New York, and that was what mattered. There was no question of my living on campus because MSM had no dorms back then. But I found an apartment before the semester was three days old, in the same quasi-magical way I'd picked a conservatory. I visited the dean of students, Josephine Whitford, a small, plump woman somewhere in her sixties (soft, kindly face; soft gray pompadour), whose job was to be Mother Hen to the whole enormous brood of us. She immediately led me out of her office and down the stairs of the glass dining pavilion (hen-like, hop, hop, hop), calling out, "Here's someone who needs a roommate!" She was calling to someone named Carol, and just like that, for $140 a month, I acquired a room in a furnished apartment up the street on Claremont Avenue.

The place looked grungy even when it was clean: a fourth-floor walkup with two small bedrooms, a kitchen with a tiny table shoehorned in, and a bathroom where neither grout nor porcelain could be scrubbed white, not that I tried. ("I wouldn't walk in there barefoot for *money*," said Mother.) The front door was encumbered with something called a police lock. I'd never seen anything like it: a steel rod running diagonally from a cast-iron lockbox above the doorknob to a slot in the floor, bracing the door shut. You opened it from outside with a key that slid the rod to one side so it could move freely, making a sound like a jail-cell door. What kind of neighborhood required that level of security?

The apartment was dark, though each room had a good-sized window. There was no safe way to wash the outside glass, which got filthy fast. The kitchen, living room, and my bedroom all faced what could generously be called a courtyard but was more of a glorified air shaft between two buildings. All you saw from any window was other windows, strangely blank. From my building came sounds of students practicing; in the adjacent building, radios blasted Dominican and Puerto Rican music.

I had to learn how to walk into the kitchen at night: turn on the light and close my eyes till the roaches scattered. I could live with knowing they were there if I didn't see them. That in itself was something new. I'd never seen a roach before, or imagined living in a city that was so dirty and noisy and unsafe, where streetlights delineated a yellow concrete landscape at night and there were no visible stars. I found a whole lot to hate about New York, yet I didn't hate it.

I made friends—starting with Carol, who was easy to talk to and live with. She worked as a secretary at the school and was the same sort of obsessive listener I was. When she fell in love with a recording of the ten Beethoven violin sonatas (Francescatti and Casadesus, live, at the Library of Congress), so did I. It became our soundtrack.

Carol introduced me to our downstairs neighbors, Barry (a violinist) and Charles (a violist), both MSM students. Charles was English, from an old Guernsey family. He possessed fine old silver, a few good pieces of antique furniture, and a Yorkshire terrier named Nellie. Barry was from the Bronx and owned no antiques but had acquired a Great Dane named Maude who climbed on the antique furniture and did it no good. Carol and I had a standing date to watch *Star Trek* reruns at their place at six o'clock. Barry was open, warm, and good-looking, but I deliberately fixated on Charles, who wasn't at all my type, being skinny and fastidious and, I was pretty sure, closeted. He was charming in his guarded English way, and he radiated unavailability. So I guess he *was* my type.

There was a soprano on my floor, across the airshaft, a coloratura who worked endlessly on one of the Queen of the Night's arias from The Magic Flute. I'd hear her trying to nail those high Fs at all hours. I wasn't interested in getting to know her, but I made it a point to introduce myself to the pianist one flight up, who played Liszt and Fauré on an upright that refused to stay in tune. Juliet didn't go to MSM. She studied piano privately, worked full-time, and absolutely hated the city. (The dirt, the noise, the roaches, the dearth of stars.) But she taught me something about what it meant to be a New Yorker, throwing extravagant low-budget dinner parties, taking advantage of the affordable culture all around us. Her older sister lived at a Zen Buddhist center on the East Side, and we spent New Year's Eve there, chanting the old year out and the new one in.

Every day or so, Dean Whitford would bounce down the stairs of the dining pavilion singing out an offer of free concert or opera tickets, usually donated at the last minute. This was how I learned to love Carnegie Hall, where Alfred Brendel taught me how a pianist can express the entire structure of a piece in a single phrase—an auditory hologram. It was also how I learned that in the topmost balcony of the Metropolitan Opera, so high I could touch the gold-leafed ceiling, I could hear every note perfectly, though I could barely make out the singers onstage. And that even in Row 5 of the orchestra with perfect sightlines, I couldn't stay awake through Götterdämmerung.

I didn't forge deep friendships with my fellow voice majors, though I liked them well enough. We were thrown together in lots of classes: music theory and history, sight singing, movement, ensembles large and small, and the whole flight of diction courses (Italian, German, English, French). Not a bad education, really. A singer needs all those things. But what she needs, first and foremost, is a voice people want to hear. I became less and less interested in having anyone hear mine.

My usual escape hatch, obsessive piano practice, had snapped shut. There was no piano in my apartment, and the school didn't have enough practice rooms to give me reliable access to an instrument. Lucille Sack had arranged for me to study with the celebrated teacher Robert Goldsand, but I stopped the lessons after a semester, though he was gracious, and I respected him enormously. It was too mortifying to walk into his studio unprepared.

I needed to be seized. That was my life story: falling madly in love with someone or something and being drawn or driven by it. I couldn't move under my own power unless galvanized by an outside force. Without one, I drifted.

The more I studied singing, the less I felt like a singer. But I was full of song. I didn't know what that song was but knew it was imperative that I find it. I navigated by a kind of emotional sonar, sending out pings and waiting for something to ping back. Something did, from medieval Tuscany.

58

DANTE

I'D SIGNED UP FOR A LITERATURE SURVEY COURSE offered by the "Academic Department"—a catchall for everything at the school that wasn't music (excluding math and science, which didn't exist there). It was taught by John Saly, head of the department and its one full-time professor. The first book on the syllabus was Dante's *Inferno*, which I hadn't read.

Dr. Saly began with a dry explanation of the three levels of allegory in the Divine Comedy: sociopolitical allegory, reflecting the society of Dante's time; moral allegory, tracing the individual's path out of sin to purification and grace; and spiritual allegory, the deeper story of the soul's journey from isolation to oneness with God.

Oh dear, I thought. *This is going to be way too complicated.*

But it wasn't. Though I had a passing interest in the political references, I didn't try very hard to find my way around fourteenth-century Florence. It was the soul's journey that transfixed me—the idea that there was a path to self-understanding, and I was on it. I believed this, knew it intuitively. In a class of music majors grappling with a late-medieval epic and trying to suss out what would be on the exam, I was the one taking it personally.

We read the poem in a prose translation with the Italian on the facing pages. I understood enough Italian to appreciate the music of the poetry—its elegant *terza rima* stanzas, its diction ranging from the gritty vernacular to the exalted. Even in the more difficult passages, I found it beautiful.

Dr. Saly was Hungarian—of course!—maybe fifty, tall, sharp-eyed, and lean. His accent was almost as thick as Sebök's but less musical; his classroom voice was angular, even harsh—a voice better suited to talking softly, person to person. When he sensed the class was inattentive, his discomfort would become palpable. Even at his most relaxed, he was nervous, intent on self-expression. He gestured, drew diagrams, made faces, summoned all his powers of analogy. Dr. Saly had things to say. It was clear the path of self-discovery was personal for him too.

You don't set out on that path. You find yourself on it, as Dante finds himself in a dark wood at the poem's beginning. His path leads through hell, where quite a few spiritual journeys begin.

The souls in *Inferno* go around in circles, endlessly, with no way out—because, as Dr. Saly pointed out, they are estranged from themselves. They refuse to acknowledge their own pride or anger or cruelty or avarice or lust—which are revealed to be sins against the self—and so remain trapped in them forever.

Dante finds his way out of hell by descending to its lowest depths, guided by the poet Virgil, who personifies Reason. He sees tormented souls—the torments are graphic and sensational—in increasing states of alienation: the malignant growth of the ego, the death of feeling, the corruption of relationships between self and other, self and self—leading, ultimately, to spiritual death. The bottom of hell is frozen. Satan—Lucifer, the angel who fell farthest from heaven—is a bat-winged, three-headed giant trapped waist-deep in ice. Dante and Virgil grasp his matted fur and climb downward, until—having gone as far down as they can go—they find themselves climbing upward, toward Purgatory. That's how *Inferno* ends, in a cliffhanger.

When we got to this point, Dr. Saly asked us if we'd like to read *Purgatorio* and *Paradiso* instead of the other books on the syllabus. I said yes, emphatically. Nobody else said no.

Purgatory—what a relief!—is a realm of light and quiet: not many souls have been there. In this place, Dr. Saly said, the self has been broken open, and one must summon the will to continue. There's punishment for sins in Purgatory, but the punishments are longed for and received in joy, because they are the way to God. Sinners move not in circles but in an upward spiral: they face the same aspects of themselves over and over, but it gets easier to forgive themselves as they are forgiven. Take the words *God* and *sin* out of this, and you have a fair description of psychotherapy.

Purgatory, said Dr. Saly, is about the purification of the will. At the summit, Virgil leaves Dante, telling him that from this point on, he can be guided by whatever gives him pleasure: *lo tuo piacere omai prendi per duce*. That passage leaped out at me—not because Dante is being told to follow his bliss, but because of everything he's had to go through to get to this point. It's terribly easy to believe that something, or someone, will make you happy. It's much harder to learn how you get in the way of your own happiness, to learn what your happiness is. It's a life's work.

Paradiso is about the soul turning toward truth, learning to ask questions, learning to love. Dante's guide there is Beatrice, the transformative figure he met just twice in real life. I understood her, having had a Beatrice of my own. *Paradiso* is a literary acid trip, with all the blessed souls, saints, and angels moving like clockwork in their divine spheres, culminating in a beatific vision. Not the most accessible part of the poem. It's where Dante builds his true church, and even in those days, I never walked into any church without walking out again.

But the idea of *l'amor che move il sole e l'altre stele*—love that moves the sun and the other stars, love as the force that binds the universe together—that felt real.

We did a strange dance that semester, Dr. Saly and I. Sometimes I felt he was addressing me directly, that we had a kinship. But I had neither the nerve nor the opportunity to talk to him outside the classroom. I felt something for him, not a romantic something, but strong, and it puzzled me. I eventually managed to tell him that, after his classes, I felt as if I could walk through walls, as if there were no walls. It was a sort of declaration, I suppose, but he took it in stride. Dante could evoke that kind of response.

What was happening to me? Was I looking for God? If so, which God?

I pondered this over the next few months, back in Syracuse for one last summer. My father was now the physician at the local Chrysler plant that made auto transmissions. Without exactly consulting me, he got me a job on the assembly line—my first real job, and another sort of revelation entirely. I started on the night shift and still shudder to think about the people that drove the cars whose brakes I inspected. The noise of the place was overwhelming: endless clanging and riveting, the harsh whine of gears being cut, alarms ringing out as the line started and stopped. Huge open furnaces roared through the hot summer nights; everything smelled and tasted of metal and sweat. I read my copy of *Inferno* on the 3:00 a.m. lunch breaks.

I couldn't stop thinking about the journey through Purgatory as Dr. Saly had described it: a process of being stripped of illusions, dropping the mask of self-importance, and acknowledging your own capacity for evil. Of facing your inner chaos and knowing it can be resolved.

Back in Manhattan and wanting a fresh start at seeing myself, I decided to avoid mirrors for a while. I hadn't realized

how many mirrors there were—every storefront, every win-
dowpane, every puddle; the toaster, the coffeepot, the back of a
spoon. All I did in life, it seemed, was sneak glances at myself.
Not doing so was a great challenge, but I figured that if my
blind friend Susan could groom herself perfectly well in the
dark, so could I. I managed it for two whole months, at the end
of which I positioned myself before the full-length mirror in
Carol's room and opened my eyes.

I was rewarded with thirty seconds of encountering myself
for the first time. The newness wore off after that. I wasn't fat.
Dressed in a borrowed lace leotard and straight skirt, I was
shapely, pleasing to look at, even pretty—with calm, serious
green eyes and a thick curtain of dark blonde hair. And—my
goodness—I *did* have a long face. No wonder people told me I
reminded them of portraits by Modigliani. You'd think I'd have
noticed.

59

DRUMMIE

WAS ANN DRUMMOND-GRANT STILL WITH ME? Always. Especially in moments like this, when I took quiet stock of myself. She was there in the silence. I was beginning to be aware that when I felt a presence—watching me, or just being with me—I could ascribe it to anyone. I could say it was God, though by this time I was irritated by the notion of a Heavenly Father barging in on me. I could say it was whoever I was obsessed with at the moment. Whoever I wanted to talk to, living or dead. I could say it was my own greater self, too large and multidimensional for this human body. Silence can hold all *kinds* of people.

But I was careful with Drummie. I didn't want to make her into a mascot. She was something more important, something holy. And you can't, you mustn't try to pin down holiness. It vibrates. Fix it in place, and it dies.

If Drummie had lived, and I'd written to her, and she'd written back—one of the countless gracious notes she wrote to fans—and given me motherly advice and encouragement, as was her way, she'd have become one more person in my life, and I'd have learned how much we had to say to each other. None of that would have had anything to do with the thrill of her voice. The vibration of it that somehow lived on. When I dreamed of her, not often, but always significantly, it was about finding a new photo of her, a new recording, some new way of encountering her. She was gone, but she was there.

She seemed to have died mysteriously, unexpectedly. Or so I'd read in a 1973 article about her in *The Savoyard*, the D'Oyly Carte's little magazine: "On September 11, 1959, the world of Gilbert and Sullivan was shocked and stunned to hear that she had died on that day. It was announced over the radio and on TV, and, although many of us knew she was ill, we were not prepared or ready for her untimely death."

For a long time, I romanticized this. Everyone expected her to return, but she slipped away like a will-o'-the-wisp. I was over fifty when I saw her death certificate. There was no slipping involved. Drummie died of breast cancer, and it took years to kill her—during which time she simply kept performing, in glorious voice, reliable as ever. She made only one concession to her illness that I know of, in Lady Jane's second-act duet with Bunthorne in *Patience*. There was a bit in one of the encores where she carried Bunthorne offstage, piggyback. In her last season she no longer had the strength for that.

"When the company played its winter season in the West End in 1958–59, her health was causing her friends much anxiety," said a London obituary. "But she refused to rest, and it was by a remarkable effort of willpower that she was able to carry on until the end of the season." Actors have a phrase for this: Doctor Theatre. You can feel like you're at death's door, but you make a miraculous recovery when the curtain goes up, only to relapse when it comes back down.

I'm sure it was more than willpower that kept her going. The physical act of warming up before a performance, waking that enormous voice, the low notes resonating upward through the chest, the shimmering top notes vibrating in the face and behind the eyes, the voice spinning outward, filling the dressing room in a towering column of sound: it was her presence in the world. It was personhood.

Because she was so resilient, so strong-willed, and so *dignified* (a word almost invariably used to describe her), it's difficult to chart the course of her illness with certainty. It seems probable that the first sign of it was in 1956, during the American tour, around the time the nurse in New York speculated that "Miss Grant might be unwell." Her colleague Jon Ellison recalled that she wasn't in her normal good health at the end of that tour, "but in those days cancer was rather a forbidden subject, and a shroud of secrecy covered Drummie's condition." Was she treated for breast cancer that spring? It would have meant surgery or radiation; she seems never to have had a mastectomy. *Something* happened. And then she was fine.

She had two more good years. Her great recordings of *Mikado* and *Pirates* were made in 1957. But in September 1958, Tony Joseph—he who used to watch her greeting fans outside the stage door—had a letter from his friend Tony Gower: "I learned that Drummie is ill, and I am sorry to say very seriously ill. She is either due to have, or has had, an abdominal operation and will be out of the company for some considerable time."

She was out for three months, convalescing with her sister in Edinburgh while Goddie toured with the company. Early in December, Tony Joseph had another letter: "Oh, joy! Drummie is again quite fit and started in Liverpool last week, and I saw her myself going into the Princes [Theatre, in London] today." She seemed in top form; her reviews were glowing, as always. On the BBC radio broadcast of *The Gondoliers* from January 1959, she sounds hearty and indomitable.

She wasn't. By late spring, she was done. Her final performance was as Katisha, in Bournemouth, on May 23. She believed she might return to work even then. She believed it almost to the end, and so did her husband. If belief were enough, she'd be here still.

Her D'Oyly Carte compatriots saw only the outer edges of her illness, but what they saw was dire enough. They were alerted to her condition when a performer with whom she shared a dressing room noticed a lump on Drummie's breast. A visible lump. Drummie must have known it was there. Maybe she didn't want to know. There was a perception among some of her colleagues that she had delayed getting proper medical attention—that her death soon afterward was partly her fault. None of them knew what she went through in the last year of her life.

I know something about it now, having seen a letter Isidore Godfrey wrote to a family friend in August 1959. The letter lay in a collector's archive for decades and surfaced just as I was finishing this book. I felt—couldn't help feeling—that Goddie wanted me to have the whole story.

In the fall of 1958, Drummie underwent a course of deep radiation therapy. Goddie's letter doesn't say if she also had surgery at that point, but the treatment must have been grueling; it took three months out of her life. It was deemed successful. She was able to work through the London season and beyond. But then "the trouble burst out again, and worse than before." This would have been around the time the visible lump was discovered. More radiation followed, to no avail. "So she had to pack up and go into hospital, where she received a further two different and very painful treatments," Goddie wrote. "These did not help either." The radiation left her so anemic she needed six pints of blood.

Then she got a reprieve. Goddie took her to Cornwall for two weeks, and her sister Agnes came to look after her. She enjoyed this. But as soon as she got back to London, she had surgery to remove her adrenal glands, where breast cancer sometimes spreads. There may have been further surgeries. Her colleague Jeffrey Skitch visited her at the hospital and found her heavily bandaged. "I believe they removed some lymphatic vessels from her chest and underarms," he told me. None of it did any good.

Awful as this sounds, awful as it undeniably was, it probably represented the standard of care in 1959. Drummie's surgery was at an extremely posh private hospital. Bridget D'Oyly Carte must have paid for her treatment there, and quite possibly the Cornwall trip. It's the sort of gesture she regularly, quietly made.

Jon Ellison also visited. He and his wife, Joy, were close to her. Here's his account:

> I remember we were playing the Hippodrome, Golders Green, north London, when Drummie was desperately ill. I went to see her in the Lindo Wing at St. Mary's Hospital, Paddington, just two weeks before she died. She was in a small room, and I can visualise her even now, sitting up in bed, and taking the flowers I had brought, with a brave, weak smile. She was wearing a pale blue nightie, with a white knitted bed jacket, and also a hairnet. She looked a shadow of her former self, and I can remember so very clearly she had a startled, shocked, and hurt expression in her eyes, and I so sadly knew at that moment that she wasn't going to recover. We had a lovely little talk, and as I was about to leave, I gave her a little kiss on the cheek, and she grasped my hand and said, "Give my love to Joy."

I was struck by Jon's description of the look in her eyes. I thought at first that he was describing her emotional state—that she must have been furious to find herself at this pass. Now that I've lived somewhat longer, I understand she was in physical pain. I've seen that expression in the mirror and know what it signifies. But she was a D'Oyly Carter to the last: welcoming, gracious, impeccably dressed.

60

AFTER

"WHEN HER DEATH WAS ANNOUNCED, the atmosphere in the theater that night was dreadful," Jon Ellison told me. "I think we all thought she was invincible." Drummie was so dependably good, so rarely sidelined by colds or sore throats—so reliably *there*—that her absence was unfathomable. Goddie, having made a superhuman effort to keep hope alive and Drummie with it, could scarcely comprehend it. During her funeral service—packed with mourners, piled high with floral tributes—he found himself unable to think or speak. "I still cannot believe all that has happened—it does not seem possible," he wrote to that same family friend. "My great consolation is that Drum now is suffering no more pain for, you know, she did suffer and fought so bravely even when she was working. . . ."

By the time I learned that she died of breast cancer, I knew several women who'd been cured of it. I know more survivors now, women who went into treatment reasonably assured of good outcomes. I've also known women who died of it, but it's no longer an automatic death sentence. I imagine saying to Drummie: "They can cure this now." And what does that have to do with the course of her life? Nothing. She lived to work and worked till the last possible minute. She fought for the career she wanted, lost it, regained it, lost it again. Fought like mad to live. Her death came as an enormous shock to those who knew and loved her—and to me, nine years after the fact.

This was a powerful woman. I understood that when I first encountered her as a disembodied voice, soaring and impassioned, demanding to be heard. She was my friend and protector, my source of solace and joy. She, personally. And I felt bound to look after her as she looked after me.

But this was also the quiet, unassuming woman who made sure her husband always had clean dress shirts for work; who lived in a spacious house in Cricklewood with a nice back garden; who loved a fearless and notoriously flatulent little dog that trotted after her wherever she went; who liked to cook and poured a generous "wee dram" of Scotch for her guests. Who tended to see the dark side of things, having known darkness early, but also found humor in it. Who radiated a kind of serenity because she had a life she loved. All this matters more than the fact that she died too young.

Her replacement in the company, Gillian Knight, was twenty-five and barely out of music school when she auditioned for the job. She was told it was temporary: Drummie, being invincible, would return. But it was Gillian Knight who recorded the role of Little Buttercup in August 1959, and then had to learn six contralto roles at lightning speed. Her new colleagues rallied to support her, and she slipped neatly into her place in the D'Oyly Carte machine—though she was so willowy her costumes had to be fitted with long sleeves to hide her slender arms. She acquitted herself magnificently.

Isidore Godfrey would have rehearsed her in those contralto roles and looked up from the orchestra pit to see her onstage. He carried on, of course, but according to Jon Ellison, a vital spark had gone out of him.

After her death he was completely shattered, really a lost soul. It was heartrending to see him walk into the theatre with Dougal. I don't think he ever got over her death. His next marriage, though I'm sure not the love match he enjoyed with Drummie, certainly saved him. I remember he came with his new wife to our home on one occasion, and he talked, with misting eyes, about "Drum."

I'm told that Mary Godfrey, the "new wife," had been a lifelong friend. I know she was Jewish because someone who attended their wedding reception in 1961 told me they were married in a synagogue. I believe this would have been a comfort to him. She would have had a certain specific understanding of who he was and where he came from. And I gather that she, too, took very good care of him. He died on September 12, 1977, eighteen years and a day after Drummie's death.

61

THE PURGATORY
THING

In February 1975, toward the beginning of my third
semester at the Manhattan School of Music, I read Martyn
Green's long and impressive obituary in the *New York Times*. It
gave me a proprietary feeling; he had, after all, been part of my
life. I remembered how he had discouraged my ambition to join
the D'Oyly Carte and how determined I'd been to prove him
wrong. Now both the ambition and the determination seemed
distant, almost quaint. I'd been studying singing for six long
years without really getting anywhere. I sang all the time—
most of my classes involved performing in some fashion—but
took scant joy in it. Something else was preoccupying me.

It was the Purgatory thing, the desire to untangle myself
and see myself plain. I wouldn't have put it that way. I knew
only that Dante's great poem had left me in a state of hunger.
Sometimes I thought I was hungering for God—I'd begun to
read everything I could about mystics and mysticism. But reli-
gion as I understood it meant submitting to an outside force,
and this wasn't that.

Whatever it was, it *felt* religious: powerful, vibratory. I
started having dreams that felt important, or at least urgent.
Dreams where I wandered the subway system, or opened my

front door to find strangers, menacing or benign, trying to gain entrance. The kinds of dreams people have when they start poking around in their own subconscious.

I was twenty-one, vocationally dead-ended, still a virgin. It would have been a logical point in my life to go into therapy—or, given my temperament, to follow my neighbor Juliet's older sister into Zen Buddhism and sit in silence, pondering, or not pondering, unanswerable questions. I did neither. But in a way, I did both: I joined a spiritual community that practiced a rigorous introspection that was, in effect, therapy. I came to it through Dr. Saly, who told me about it after much hesitation. If it had been anyone else, I wouldn't have gone near it. I wasn't looking for any kind of community, let alone a spiritual one.

The Pathwork was one of the New Age groups that flourished during the seventies, though this particular group had been around for years. The term "New Age" could signify many things: crystal healing, spirit guides, rebirthing therapy, and generally going off the deep end. The Pathwork's teachings came from a spirit guide, channeled through a trance medium. This was about as far off the deep end as a person could go, and I understood why Dr. Saly hadn't rushed to tell me about it.

The trance medium, Eva Pierrakos, was a Viennese expat from a literary family, centered and forthright, with a gift for cutting to the chase. I found her teachings deeply practical. They were about taking responsibility for your life instead of blaming others for your problems, seeking an inner truth that could be trusted—a God Within, as opposed to a Daddy God.

There's a kind of self-honesty where you beat yourself up and revel in it, and another kind where you acknowledge your own contribution to unhappy situations. The former kind gets you nowhere. The latter kind is liberating. That's the simplest possible explanation of what I learned in the Path: that it was safe to look at the parts of myself I was afraid to see—my fears and judgments and (especially) my anger. Basic human feelings I needed to experience and understand.

Maybe I wasn't so great at singing. But after years of writing everything down, I was good at introspection. I could look at myself and cop to what was right in front of me. The Pathwork was churchy, in that it involved meditation and prayer, but it was a church of self-improvement, a very 1970s sort of edifice. The whole group was committed to self-honesty, and it could get pretty intense; there were conflicts, power struggles, lapses of judgment. But it was also enormously joyful. All these years after leaving the Path, I'm still grateful for what I learned there.

There were about three hundred people in the community, mostly white and affluent, or aspiring to affluence. That was the rub: it wasn't free. There were various therapeutic sessions and groups, all of which cost money. Some took place at a Center in the Catskills, where room and board had to be paid or worked for. If I wanted to take part in this, I realized, I'd have to find a way to make a living, since singing was not an art I was willing to starve for.

62

MRS. RASKIN

Around this time, paradoxically, my singing improved. I managed to get myself assigned to a teacher who had just joined the faculty, the soprano Judith Raskin. I adored her. If I'd bestirred myself to find out more about her, I'd have learned that she had a distinguished operatic and concert career, but all I knew was that I had once hung a poster of her on my bedroom wall because she reminded me of Ann Drummond-Grant. Something about the solitary way she stood. She was shorter than Drummie, small and shapely, with dark, curly hair framing a valentine of a face—the perfect Susanna or Zerlina, to name two of her signature Mozart roles.

When I met her, she was in her midforties and a breast cancer survivor—in her case, a visible thing. She'd had a radical mastectomy, and her right arm was swollen to the fingertips with chronic lymphedema. I'm sure it was uncomfortable, though she carried herself gracefully. I didn't understand that her illness had interrupted her career, basically stopped it cold; I only gathered there were vocal difficulties of some sort. And that this somehow made her more compassionate about my difficulties.

I spent a year and a half with Judy—I don't think I ever called her that, but I'm sure she wouldn't have minded. We were comfortable with each other. She had consoled me when

I had a meltdown after a disastrous date. (I'd finally started going out with men and had no idea what I was doing.) And she'd confided in me when she lost a favorite aunt to cancer. So many women in her family had died of it, she said, allowing a bleakness to glaze her eyes. If it had been 2006 and not 1976, she'd have known about the gene she carried and might have dodged the ovarian cancer that killed her at fifty-six. I know this is a useless thought, but I hate the way it cut her down.

Judy—Mrs. Raskin—heard the problems in my voice and was determined to fix them. She had me use the lowest part of my voice, the strong, deep notes of the chest register, to open my throat so the higher notes could be more properly placed. It helped. My voice became fuller from top to bottom, though I was still missing the essential component of proper breath support. What helped most was that she actually cared about me and encouraged me. When she demonstrated the right way to sing a phrase—her voice was silvery, radiant, like a cascade of moonlight—I learned by imitating her. If I shaped the vowels as she shaped them, my voice would shine. It was a note-by-note victory, success in tiny increments.

She and I both knew I wasn't destined for a singing career. It was enough that she prepared me for my senior recital. That was actually fun: putting together a program with the requisite groupings in German, Italian, English, and French, consisting of songs I could actually sing. Brahms, Mozart, Britten, Gounod. It was like being a bride—everything was about me for that one event.

I was easing my way out of school by this time, having finished my course requirements except for the voice lessons. Since I'd transferred to the school as a freshman, there was no way my parents could avoid paying four years of tuition. They'd had to take out a loan to do it, and I realized I needed to become financially independent. Through a Pathwork friend, I'd gotten a part-time secretarial job. The paycheck was meager, but it was magic: it bought freedom and self-respect. Before the year was over, I had a full-time job that paid not much more but enabled me, with a little moonlighting, to let my parents off the hook. They were stunned.

The recital was my first and only solo concert. I had great luck with it, and great pleasure. Mrs. Raskin was part of the luck, and so was my pianist/coach, Tom Grubb. He was my French diction teacher—French diction is incredibly fussy—and had accompanied many famous singers in recital, including Elly Ameling. I felt honored when he decided to play for me instead of having a piano student do it. It was the difference between walking a tightrope and riding in a chauffeured limousine.

Mrs. Raskin told me afterward that I gave one of those recitals where the singer becomes more and more relaxed and the voice just blooms. I guess I was finally able to let go of everything except making music. I had nothing to prove. The recital hall—the same hall where I'd sung such a bad audition—was full of friends and family who were glad to be there. And I was glad to sing for them.

My encore was for Drummie. The article in *The Savoyard* had described an evening many years ago, when the D'Oyly Carte were on tour in Edinburgh. "They . . . made a social call at one of the Edinburgh clubs, and as usual when the company were together on a night out, songs from the operas were sung. Miss Drummond-Grant went over to the pianist, and after giving him some music, she turned and sang to us 'Annie Laurie,' in quite a different arrangement from the usual ballad, and her beautifully rich contralto rang out, thrilling us all; everyone in the club was touched and moved to tears of joy after she had sung."

I had no idea what that "different arrangement" might have sounded like. I found the plainest, simplest version of "Annie Laurie" and prepared it, not telling anyone why. I sang it for Drummie's sake, and I sang it well. And that was that.

63

GOLDERS GREEN

The D'Oyly Carte Company gave its final performance in February 1982. Many factors contributed to its demise, but the short version is that it ran out of money, and the Arts Council, which supported most theatrical companies in Britain, refused to fund it. The council claimed that the D'Oyly Carte's performances were so tired and wooden that it was effectively dead already. There was truth to that. But a lot of the tiredness came from the company having been cash-strapped for years. It still had legions of passionately devoted fans. The council might almost have been quoting Yogi Berra: "Nobody ever goes there anymore—it's too crowded."

I noted its passing with a twinge. I was twenty-eight and had embarked on a series of jobs where I got paid to write. As Drummie had done before me, I was living with a married man, waiting for his divorce to come through. That's how I know what it had been like for her: my husband and I wanted to be together, and in due course we were and still are. My unavailable man surprised me by becoming available.

I had no regrets about the road not taken because I couldn't have taken it. But Drummie kept singing in my mind's ear and showing up in my dreams, returning on her own schedule, my comet. She was with me in 1988 when, at thirty-five, I felt compelled to take voice lessons again. I had to know if I could have been a singer after all. Somehow, by the sort of magic I'd once relied on, I found my way to Sam Sakarian, the master teacher who finally taught me the basics. I was amazed to hear my true sound emerge at last: a lyric soprano, yes, but fuller and richer than the thin, patchy one I'd despaired of for so long. At its best, a sound like burnished silver. I could have done something with that sound.

It was too late. I was just beginning to grasp the mechanics of singing. If I'd reached this point in my teens, I could have embarked on the years of training it would have taken to master my instrument. But I was pushing forty, building a career as a writer and editor—doing work I liked, generating income I needed. Was I supposed to drop everything and sing?

That's a dishonest question. Suppose I'd gotten proper training all along and been a star in music school. Suppose I'd gotten church jobs and oratorio work and even sung principal roles with one of the little G&S troupes that dotted the city back then. Just suppose. The truth is that, even if I'd forged such a career for myself, I wouldn't have stuck it out. After working with Sam for three years, I realized that even with a *good* voice, I didn't really want to stand in front of people and sing. Not even "Happy Birthday."

My true instrument turned out to be the one I made my living with, the written word. That voice, after years of practice, is everything my singing voice wasn't: supple and assured, as large or small as I need it to be. I can use it now to give something back to Drummie, who shaped my life. A singer needs a listener, and I am hers.

In 2006, I made a pilgrimage to her handsome Victorian house in northwest London. It looked shabby and rundown; there was a boarded-up broken window in front. I couldn't quite picture her living there, though I could imagine walking a small dog up and down the broad sidewalks of that quiet, orderly neighborhood. The house was later refurbished and divided into three large flats that sold for a great deal of money. Someone is breakfasting in a bright white kitchen in what used to be Drummie's attic, where sun streams in through a window overlooking the back garden.

On that same London trip, I visited Golders Green Crematorium, approximately forty-seven years late for Drummie's funeral. I'd never seen such a place, stately and cloistered as a monastery, with acres of gardens. There was a redbrick colonnade whose walls were jammed with plaques honoring the famous people incinerated there. Lush grass grew on the "sacred scattering ground," and even in November, there was a sprinkling of roses on the memorial bushes. Drummie's colleague Jon Ellison had gone to the trouble of finding out where her ashes were scattered: in a corner, next to the Winston Churchill Rose Bed. There I stood, in an interval between sun and rain. A fine black crow was walking on the lawn, and I could hear a jackhammer in the distance. But Drummie herself was gone.

Not completely gone: *I* was there.

ACKNOWLEDGMENTS

I'M GRATEFUL TO CYNTHIA MOREY, who worked closely with Ann Drummond-Grant, for allowing me to quote from her memoirs *Inclined to Dance and Sing* and *A Set of Curious Chances*. I'm also indebted to the late Jon Ellison, who took the time and trouble to write down everything he remembered about working with Drummie, bringing her to life for me as no one else could have. Copious thanks also to Roberta Morrell—writer, director, former D'Oyly Carte principal and tireless compiler of tales of the company—for her advice and support.

Thanks to Chris Webster, whose digital recordings brought me much more of Drummie's voice than I'd had before. Chris put me in touch with Tony Joseph, lifelong D'Oyly Carte fan and chronicler, who encouraged me to write this book and sent me tantalizing bits of information: records of Drummie's marriage and death, reviews from every stage of her career, even a couple of color photos. By the time I had a manuscript to show him, ill health prevented him from reading it. Tony died in 2021, way too soon.

I couldn't have completed this memoir without Nell Nelson, my spirit-sister in Scotland, or Jennifer Goodrich and Stephanie Young, my stalwart first readers in the US. They read every word of every draft and kept telling me to go on. I needed that.

Anne Mazer and Molly Peacock read this book and believed in it. I needed that too.

Thanks, finally, to my husband, Ted Berk, who gave me room to write. This was no small thing.

Lyrics from *Hair* by Gerome Ragni and James Rado reprinted with permission. Background on Nottingham High from *The World We Created at Hamilton High* by Gerald Grant, Harvard University Press, Revised Edition, 1990.

Advice for young girls in Chapter 3 from *Time to Grow Up* by Candy Jones, Harper & Row, 1962.

ABOUT THE AUTHOR

Marcia Menter grew up in Syracuse, New York, and earned a degree in vocal performance from the Manhattan School of Music. She held senior writing and editing positions at national magazines including *Glamour*, *Mademoiselle*, *Self*, *Redbook*, and *More*. Her self-help book, *The Office Sutras: Exercises for Your Soul at Work*, was published in 2003 by Red Wheel/Weiser Press. Her poetry chapbook, *The Longing Machine*, was published in 2007 by HappenStance Press in Scotland. She has contributed poems, essays, and literary criticism to journals in the US and UK. She lives in Manhattan.

SELECTED TITLES FROM SHE WRITES PRESS

She Writes Press is an independent publishing company
founded to serve women writers everywhere.
Visit us at www.shewritespress.com.

Shedding Our Stars: The Story of Hans Calmeyer and How He Saved Thousands of Families Like Mine by Laureen Nussbaum with Karen Kirtley. $16.95, 978-1-63152-636-7. From his post at the headquarters of the German occupation during World War II, Hans Calmeyer surreptitiously saved thousands of Jewish lives in the Netherlands. Here, Laureen Nussbaum describes how Calmeyer declared her mother non-Jewish and deleted her and her family from the deportation lists—and traces the arc of both her life and Calmeyer's in the aftermath of the war.

Twentieth-Century Boys: How One Multigenerational Family Business Survived and Thrived by Andrea Clark Watson. $16.95, 978-1-64742-317-9. Early in the twentieth century, families lured by American business entrepreneurship immigrated to the United States—but only some of the resulting businesses survived the Great Depression and America's entry into World War II. *Twentieth-Century Boys* is about one of those family businesses and how it changed in order to survive through three generations and countless national crises.

Api's Berlin Diaries: My Quest to Understand My Grandfather's Nazi Past by Gabrielle Robinson. $16.95, 978-1-64742-003-1. After her mother's death, Gabrielle Robinson found diaries her grandfather had kept while serving as doctor in Berlin 1945—only to discover that her beloved "Api" had been a Nazi.

Jumping Over Shadows: A Memoir by Annette Gendler. $16.95, 978-1-63152-170-6. Like her great-aunt Resi, Annette Gendler, a German, fell in love with a Jewish man—but unlike her aunt, whose marriage was destroyed by "the Nazi times," Gendler found a way to make her impossible love survive.

When a Toy Dog Became a Wolf and the Moon Broke Curfew: A Memoir by Hendrika de Vries. $16.95, 978-1631526589. Hendrika is "Daddy's little girl," but when Nazis occupy Amsterdam and her father is deported to a POW labor camp, she must bond with her mother—who joins the Resistance after her husband's deportation—and learn about female strength in order to discover the strong woman she can become.